**New Directions for
Adult and Continuing
Education**

Susan Imel
Jovita M. Ross-Gordon
COEDITORS-IN-CHIEF

Adult Learning and the Emotional Self

John M. Dirkx
EDITOR

Number 120 • Winter 2008
Jossey-Bass
San Francisco

ADULT LEARNING AND THE EMOTIONAL SELF
John M. Dirkx (ed.)
New Directions for Adult and Continuing Education, no. 120
Susan Imel, Jovita M. Ross-Gordon, Coeditors-in-Chief

Microfilm copies of issues and articles are available in 16mm and 35mm, as well as microfiche in 105mm, through University Microfilms Inc., 300 North Zeeb Road, Ann Arbor, Michigan 48106-1346.

NEW DIRECTIONS FOR ADULT AND CONTINUING EDUCATION (ISSN 1052-2891, electronic ISSN 1536-0717) is part of The Jossey-Bass Higher and Adult Education Series and is published quarterly by Wiley Subscription Services, Inc., A Wiley Company, at Jossey-Bass, 989 Market Street, San Francisco, California 94103-1741. Periodicals Postage Paid at San Francisco, California, and at additional mailing offices. POSTMASTER: Send address changes to New Directions for Adult and Continuing Education, Jossey-Bass, 989 Market Street, San Francisco, California 94103-1741.

New Directions for Adult and Continuing Education is indexed in CIJE: Current Index to Journals in Education (ERIC); Contents Pages in Education (T&F); ERIC Database (Education Resources Information Center; Higher Education Abstracts (Claremont Graduate University); and Sociological Abstracts (CSA/CIG).

SUBSCRIPTIONS cost $89.00 for individuals and $228.00 for institutions, agencies, and libraries.

EDITORIAL CORRESPONDENCE should be sent to the Coeditors-in-Chief, Susan Imel, ERIC/ACVE, 1900 Kenny Road, Columbus, Ohio 43210-1090, e-mail: imel.l@osu.edu; or Jovita M. Ross-Gordon, Southwest Texas State University, EAPS Dept., 601 University Drive, San Marcos, TX 78666.

Cover photograph by Jack Hollingsworth@Photodisc

www.josseybass.com

CONTENTS

EDITOR'S NOTES

"What is infinity?" the teacher asked Billy, a somewhat troubled young learner in third grade. After being quiet for a moment, Billy responded excitedly, "Infinity is like a box of Cream of Wheat!" Many of us might remember, back in the days when this cereal was more popular, that adorning the front of the Cream of Wheat box was a man holding a box of Cream of Wheat. For that insightful and creative response, however, Billy was sent to the principal's office (Jones, 1968) and eventually the school counselor.

Although Jones's text is now forty years old, it remains a powerful representation of the role of fantasy, feeling, and emotion in education. Unfortunately, Billy's fate illustrates how their expression within educational contexts is often misinterpreted and misunderstood. A deeper understanding of feelings and emotions is no less important to adult learners than it is to third-grade boys.

For many years, I have been interested in the psychosocial or emotional dimensions of adult learning. Although I was professionally prepared in a previous life as a clinical microbiologist, I never accepted that learning was strictly or even primarily a cognitive event or process. Perhaps it is the Billy in me, but learning has always been intimately bound up with making sense of what it is I am trying to learn, in the light of my own experiences and the world around me. This meaning-making process reflects, in a fundamental way, my emotional engagement with the text, or the focus of my learning. But it also reveals my relationship with others who make up the broader social and cultural context in which my learning is occurring.

But what do we really mean by emotion and, in particular, what does it mean within settings of adult learning? The emotional or affective dimensions of our lives have long been a focus and concern of scholars. A large, diverse, and distinguished body of literature gives testimony to its pervasive and interdisciplinary influence in the arts and sciences. Recently, however, scholars have increasingly turned their attention to understanding the presence of emotion within a variety of organizational contexts, including organizations, the workplace, and contexts for teaching and learning (Linnenbrink, 2006). Spurred by Daniel Goleman's popularization of emotional intelligence (1995), many are now using the idea of emotion to probe the personal, social, and cultural fabric of human existence further.

Goleman's work caught our collective imagination in ways few intellectual ideas do. It signaled a pronounced shift in our attitudes toward emotion, from one in which emotion was regarded as roughly equivalent to unwanted bile circulating within our being, to a recognition of its

WILEY InterScience®
DISCOVER SOMETHING GREAT

NEW DIRECTIONS FOR ADULT AND CONTINUING EDUCATION, no. 120, Winter 2008 © 2008 Wiley Periodicals, Inc.
Published online in Wiley InterScience (www.interscience.wiley.com) • DOI: 10.1002/ace.310

constructive and intelligent role in most meaningful human endeavors. Attending to the constructive and creative influence of affect is now regarded by many as a critical dimension of the work of the mainstream scientist, as well as the avant-garde artist. Although many still view emotion as something to be carefully monitored and kept in check, we have begun to witness a more nuanced understanding of its influence in individual and collective life.

Adult learning remains an area of theory and practice in which we are only beginning to attend to the powerful role that emotion plays in our lives. Although previous volumes of *New Directions for Adult and Continuing Education* have featured chapters on emotional and affective dimensions of adult learning, none features this topic as its central focus. These dimensions are, however, reflected in a growing body of scholarship within adult learning and related fields. Writers such as Merriam, Caffarella, and Baumgartner (2007) and Tennant (1997) are giving more space to a discussion of the role that emotion plays in adult learning. Explorations of the spiritual (English, Fenwick, and Parsons, 2003; Tisdell, 2003) and transformative dimensions (Cranton, 2006, O'Sullivan, 1999) of adult learning include attempts to integrate emotion with a deeper understanding of the human condition. Even studies in organizational behavior (Stapley, 2006) and the interrelationship of work and identity (Whyte, 2002) now feature explorations of the emotional as integral avenues of their inquiry.

This volume seeks to build on this emerging scholarship by focusing on the emotional self in adult learning and the various ways in which it materializes and is expressed across a range of practice settings in adult and continuing education. These chapters also demonstrate, in different ways, the growing integration of emotion into more holistic and constructivist ways of knowing. In Chapter One, I describe the various ways in which emotions in adult learning have come to be understood, and argue that this understanding is demonstrating a profound shift in our appreciation of the emotional self in adult learning.

Perhaps no other area in adult and continuing education expresses the powerful role of emotion in teaching and learning more clearly than programs that address the needs and interests of so-called academically underprepared adults. These programs are exemplified by those about which Janet Isserlis writes in Chapter Two, including adult literacy and basic education, instruction in English as a second or other language, preparation for the general educational development diploma, and developmental education within the community college. While stressing the positive and constructive ways in which these emotional issues may contribute to a student's learning and development, Isserlis also underscores the powerful role that trauma and violence play in their lives, particularly among women students.

Higher education represents another important location for adult learning. Instrumental aims for higher education often dominate public conversations, such as meeting the needs of the workforce or the demands being created by the explosion of technology in a variety of disciplines. Yet as Carol E. Kasworm suggests in Chapter Three, the journeys of adults attending higher education often reflect varying forms of hope and expressions of a deeper engagement with their learning. For some, formal learning is something they have not done for ten to twenty years or more, and they approach the classroom with great trepidation. Adult learners also juggle many competing interests, of which education is just one. Yet in sometimes subtle ways, they often experience a reworking of their sense of self and a surge of confidence in their identity as a learner and as a person.

Online or e-learning is rapidly becoming a major setting for adult learning in higher education and an important form of learning in adulthood. Although learners are immersed in technical and virtual worlds, invisible to themselves and their teachers, proponents of e-learning stress the importance of social presence in these contexts and the development of communities of learning through collaborative and engaged activities. Yet as Regina O. Smith points out in Chapter Four, there is more here than meets the eye. When participants in e-learning try to work together collaboratively, they confront epistemic and identity issues that are emotion laden. Part of what makes an effective, collaborative online experience is learning to work across differences that can be sources of powerful affect. Compounding this work is the fact that these issues are often below the level of individual and group awareness.

In Chapter Five, Lisa M. Baumgartner and Juanita Johnson-Bailey discuss the problem of working across differences associated with race and ethnicity. Embedded in charged political environments and power relations, race and ethnicity issues within formal learning settings often evoke a range of powerful emotional issues among learners, from guilt and grief to anger and defiance. Emotions are often associated with the relations of teachers and learners within these settings, and the associated beliefs and assumptions that contribute to the construction and maintenance of their positions within the classroom.

As adults, most of us spend more time at the workplace than almost any other single context in our lives. Not only are these locations for employment and socialization; they also represent powerful contexts for adult learning and development. We have much invested in our work, yet its organization and structure, as Laura L. Bierema points out in Chapter Six, can become toxic to our overall well-being. Arising within these contexts are strong emotions associated with our relationship to the work, one another, or the broader context of the work. While some suggest the challenge is to learn to manage these emotions, Bierema opens the door for more constructive and holistic ways of understanding their presence in our work life and a fuller integration with ourselves as learners.

Extending our considerations to the imagination and the arts, Randee Lipson Lawrence in Chapter Seven challenges us to consider ways in which imaginative and artistic forms of expression might be more fully incorporated into our teaching and learning. Arts-based education, Lawrence argues, offers the potential for avenues of learning beyond what we often equate with traditional, more cognitive ways of knowing. In so doing, our learning becomes more holistic and integrated.

Looking for learning in unusual places, Edward W. Taylor in Chapter Eight reminds us of the emotional challenges that educators who work in such places as home improvement centers, parks, and museums face in engaging adults. In considering what these challenges are and how they might be addressed, Taylor suggests that emotions play a key role in getting and holding learners' attention in these diverse contexts. The task here stresses the management of what Bierema in Chapter Six refers to as emotion labor and emotion work: smiling when you feel like screaming but also using such dichotomous feelings to foster a deeper understanding of oneself.

In Chapter Nine, M. Carolyn Clark and I close the volume with further reflections on what is represented in these pages regarding the emotional self. While the previous chapter authors focused on describing the emotional dimensions of various practice settings and how such emotions contribute to more holistic and integral learning, they also implicitly give voice to several tensions, which we outline in this final chapter.

It is our collective hope that by exploring the presence and influence of emotions across a range of settings, we have contributed to an understanding of emotions as a constructive force in adult learning. Emotions, in and of themselves, are neither positive nor negative, inspiring nor brooding, illuminating nor dark and foreboding. In some instances, they are all of these, and all at the same time. By taking seriously their role in our lives and in our learning, we come to realize that such appraisals reflect more about our being-in-the-world than they do about the particular contexts in which these emotions arise. As we, as educators and students, learn to listen to our emotions and to the emotion work to which they beckon us, perhaps we will reconnect with our own emotional selves on a deeper and more meaningful level.

References

Cranton, P. *Understanding and Promoting Transformative Learning: A Guide for Educators of Adults.* San Francisco: Jossey-Bass, 2006.

English, L. M., Fenwick, T. J., and Parsons, J. *Spirituality of Adult Education and Training.* Malabar, Fla.: Krieger, 2003.

Goleman, D. *Emotional Intelligence: Why It Can Matter More Than IQ.* New York: Bantam Books, 1995.

Jones, R. M. *Fantasy and Feeling in Education.* New York: HarperCollins, 1968.

Linnenbrink, E. A. "Emotion Research in Education: Theoretical and Methodological Perspectives on the Integration of Affect, Motivation, and Cognition." *Educational Psychology Review,* 2006, *18*(4), 303–314.

Merriam, S. B., Caffarella, R. S., and Baumgartner, L. M. *Learning in Adulthood: A Comprehensive Guide.* San Francisco: Jossey-Bass, 2007.

O'Sullivan, E. *Transformative Learning: Educational Vision for the 21st Century.* London: Zed, 1999.

Stapley, L. *Individuals, Groups, and Organizations Beneath the Surface: An Introduction.* London: Karnac, 2006.

Tennant, M. *Psychology and Adult Learning.* (2nd ed.) London: Routledge, 1997.

Tisdell, E. J. *Exploring Spirituality and Culture in Adult and Higher Education.* San Francisco: Jossey-Bass, 2003.

Whyte, D. *Crossing the Unknown Sea: Work as a Pilgrimage of Identity.* New York: Riverhead Books, 2002.

John M. Dirkx
Editor

JOHN M. DIRKX is professor of higher, adult, and lifelong education at Michigan State University.

This chapter describes different ways of understanding emotions and their role in adult learning. The author suggests that our understanding of emotions is shifting from one where they are viewed as an obstacle to reason and knowing to more holistic and integral ways of knowing one's self and the world.

The Meaning and Role of Emotions in Adult Learning

John M. Dirkx

In an online graduate class in education, a middle-aged white woman wrote in her journal that she was so angry with her team members that she could have put her foot right through the computer.

On returning from a kitchen remodeling class at a home improvement store, a thirty-year-old African American man remarked that it was a great class because he felt safe enough in the context to ask what might seem to others as really stupid questions, and participating made him feel confident he could take on the home project he was planning.

A fifty-five-year-old White man, recently laid off from his manufacturing job and now in a community college developmental education math class, angrily complained to the teacher about having to learn fractions and bitterly asked her where in his world he would ever have to add and subtract fractions.

At break during a professional development conference for adult basic education, a forty-year-old Native American woman, who has been teaching in her program for fifteen years, remarked to her colleague that she really enjoyed the opportunity to hear what others were doing to address some of the problems she confronted in her teaching. She said she felt affirmed by listening to the stories of others but also excited to be able to try out some of their suggestions.

In an English Language Learning (ELL) class, the teacher, a forty-five-year-old woman of eastern European descent, was confronted with the angry outbursts of

NEW DIRECTIONS FOR ADULT AND CONTINUING EDUCATION, no. 120, Winter 2008 © 2008 Wiley Periodicals, Inc.
Published online in Wiley InterScience (www.interscience.wiley.com) • DOI: 10.1002/ace.311

one of her adult students. Later she reported that she felt herself growing very angry at this student during this episode and almost lashed out at her during class.

These brief descriptions of incidents within settings of adult learning illustrate the powerful role that emotions can play in the lives of both teachers and learners (Schutz, Hong, Cross, and Osbon, 2006). They clearly animate processes of teaching and learning and at times become so powerful that they seem to blot out virtually everything else happening at the time.

But what do these emotionally laden experiences mean? Are they aberrant blips on the landscape of adult learning, distractions from the real work of teaching and learning? Do they represent unavoidable by-products of the struggles that are part of teaching and learning and, as such, need to be accepted but their disruptive potentials minimized? Or are they somehow constitutive of the very learning processes themselves, integral to the meaning making in which the learners and the teachers are engaged? What do the emotional experiences of adults within these settings tell us about them as teachers and learners, the processes of learning, and the contexts in which these experiences occur? What role does affect have in learning?

Educators have long been interested in the role of feeling, affect, and emotion in learning (Jones, 1968; Rogers, 1969; Salzberger-Wittenberg, Henry, and Osborne, 1983), and historically adult education has recognized their importance in adult learning (Brookfield, 1986; Lindeman, 1926). Within the past fifteen to twenty years, the emotional aspects of teaching and learning in adulthood have become a major theme in the scholarly literature and professional development programs. For example, while preparing the final draft of this chapter, I received an e-mail from the National Association for Adults with Special Learning Needs announcing an upcoming webinar titled, "Emotions: Supporting the Critical Prerequisite to Learning." While emphasizing the positive contribution that emotion and affect makes on learner motivation and self-esteem, emotions are nonetheless widely recognized as a kind of baggage that impedes effective teaching and learning. As one adult learner, talking about the tensions and issues in her dislocated worker retraining group, recently told me, "Yeah, I know we are all struggling. They just need to get it off their chest, so they concentrate on getting something out of this."

Stemming from a broader discourse on emotions and the emotional self (Lewis and Haviland-Jones, 2000; Lupton, 1998), recent work in adult and continuing education reflects a re-visioning of the role of emotions in adult learning. Increasingly rejecting the notion of emotion as a barrier to reason and knowledge, this work suggests a more integral, central, and holistic role of emotion in reason, rationality, learning, and meaning making (Jarvis, 2006; Merriam, Caffarella, and Baumgartner, 2007). This volume contributes to the emerging conversation and explores various ways in which the emotional self is manifest within diverse settings of adult learning.

In doing so, we hope to honor and give voice to the importance of this often neglected dimension of adult learning.

In this chapter, I provide a brief theoretical foundation for our exploration of affect-laden experiences in adult learning. While I rely on multiple sources and disciplines to develop this overview, the study of emotions is a vast and historically situated enterprise. In these few pages, I can only acknowledge some important themes that resonate in our conversations today about and practices with adult learning. Following a brief description of the various ways affect and emotion can be expressed in the adult learning enterprise, I briefly discuss three interrelated issues: the nature and meaning of emotion, the changing understanding of the role of emotion in human experience, and the integration of emotion in adult learning.

Ways in Which Emotion Is Manifest in Adult Learning

Adult learners experience affect and emotion in a range from positive and energizing to negative and distracting. Emotions are also experienced in other ways as well, such as anger over something in the educational environment that may energize the learning experience or elation that blinds one to more difficult aspects of the experience. Learners may also experience emotions arising from within or evoked by the learning environment itself, or they may be struggling with personal issues around family, relationships, or work. Learning-related emotional issues among individuals often reflect a history of emotional experiences or trauma, of which learners may be variably aware, such as being humiliated by certain teachers in certain subjects or experiencing physical, sexual, or emotional abuse by persons in authority.

In one form or another, emotional issues never seem very far from the surface in adult learning contexts. The social and relational nature of these contexts often fosters, elicits, or implicitly encourages learners to give voice or expression to this underlying affect or emotion. Helping learners understand and make sense of these emotion-laden experiences within the context of the curriculum represents one of the most important and most challenging tasks for adult educators.

Perhaps the most common expression of strong emotions in adult learning occurs around areas of conflict, in which there may be profound disagreement of values or interest. Differences among students regarding values or interests, such as how to best proceed with a group project, often lead to feelings of anger or frustration, as in the opening example. Such emotional expressions are often bounded by the curricular contexts in which the disagreement surfaces, but they may create an affect that endures for the remainder of that particular setting or even beyond.

So-called personality conflicts among learners can result in emotional tones that color the learning experiences. For example, some learners might find the behaviors of another learner annoying in some way, and the behaviors gradually wear on them over time. Their feelings may then surprisingly erupt in powerful ways within the learning group, such as a verbal attack on the individual or indirectly on the teacher, who may be perceived as doing little or nothing about this annoying person.

Learning tasks and anticipation of being evaluated often precipitate emotional reactions among learners. They may feel anxious about doing well on a test, fear failure, or perceive themselves as unable to meet expectations. At times, the structure of the learning experience itself can foster various emotional reactions among students, some of whom may complain that not enough direction and structure are being provided, while others might feel equally strong about their being too much. Some students will express joy and elation about finally seeing the light about some problem or learning task, while others may feel overwhelmed by the multiplicity of demands within their lives. At times, students may give voice within the learning setting to the strong feelings and emotions being evoked by these various issues. Teachers may be the unwitting targets of such feelings, and they may react angrily at what they perceive as an attack on them by the students, as in the earlier example of the ELL teacher.

Occasionally curricular content stimulates powerful emotions among adult learners. For example, the subject of math often evokes considerable anxiety among many adult learners. Stories or examples included in the curriculum might bring to life for some learners painful or joyful experiences within their distant past. A teacher may precipitate affect-laden memories of earlier instructors or mentors or of one's parents. In other situations, the learning setting may simply represent a holding environment for the learners' difficult experiences within their families and relationships, or at work. These emotions often run the gamut from sadness and joy to anger and excitement.

Over twenty years ago, Brookfield (1986) characterized the adult discussion group as a psychodynamic battleground. While stretching the military metaphor a bit, Brookfield's comment underscores the profoundly emotional, affect-laden context in which adult learning occurs. The chapters in this volume suggest that the emotional contexts for adult learning and the experience of the emotional self stretch across a wide variety of settings for adult learning.

Emotion, affect, and feeling are all used to describe various aspects of these contexts. In some instances, it may be important to stress subtle differences to which these terms refer. In educational discourse, however, these terms are used fairly interchangeably, and no attempt is made in this volume to differentiate among these terms. Some emotions are experiences in a fairly focused and time-limited way within particular contexts, such as an angry reaction to being cut off in traffic or feeling insulted by what someone says in group discussion. Other emotions seem more diffuse and less restricted to particular contexts. Feeling blue or generally excited often reveals emotions about something, but we tend to have more difficulty describing just what it is we are feeling blue about or why on some days we feel so happy and upbeat. This latter form of emotional experience may be

New Directions for Adult and Continuing Education • DOI: 10.1002/ace

referred to as moods. They too are important in teaching and learning and often find expression in particular ways, such as interactions with others, our interest and motivation in learning, or the care we give to our work. Therefore, in this volume, we are interested in emotions, feelings, affect, and mood as they influence, shape, and constitute the nature and quality of adult learning experiences.

The Nature and Meaning of Emotion

The authors of the following chapters share a constructive and holistic view of emotions in adult learning. However, educators have not always looked favorably on the manifestation of emotions and feelings within the learning process. Reflecting the widespread influence of the enlightenment and the growth of scientific ways of knowing, emotions have for many years been regarded as largely undesirable within teaching and learning settings, that is, as obstacles to reason and the development of knowledge. Many educators still regard their manifestation within the learning process as a distinctly negative development, and they seek ways to avoid or mitigate their expression.

Others perceive the expression of emotions as perhaps necessary but only as a means of ventilating and allowing the learners to refocus on the learning task. Teachers who admit to this orientation suggest that it is important to let learners get things off their chest so that they may be able to devote their energies to learning what is contained within the curriculum (Dirkx and Spurgin, 1992). At the hint of affect-laden conflict, disagreement, or powerful expressions of emotionality, learners and educators alike, in many different educational contexts, tend to feel their stomach tighten, their pulse quicken, and their breathing grow more shallow and constrained. Even expressions of so-called positive emotions, such as joy or elation, are often regarded as pleasant interruptions of an otherwise sober environment.

Increasingly, however, educators are acknowledging the powerful role emotions and affect play in the adult learning process. In their widely popular text, Merriam, Caffarella, and Baumgartner (2007) demonstrate the growing recognition of emotion in various theories and models of adult learning. Jarvis (2006) devotes an entire chapter to the interrelationship of emotions and learning, suggesting that "emotions can have a considerable effect on the way we think, on motivation and on beliefs, attitudes and values" (p. 102).

Depending on whose writings you read and what discipline the scholar represents, the meaning of emotion and what is considered an emotion vary widely. Some theorists argue for a view of emotions that largely represents an innate or inherent perspective. These scholars argue that emotional states are, for the most part, physiological responses to particular stimuli, as evidenced in the flight-or-fight response to situations that evoke fear (Lupton, 1998). They are, in effect, manifestations of the lower parts of our brains

(Jarvis, 2006; Lupton, 1996). In a simplistic sense, an unanticipated encounter with a mountain lion along a quiet bubbling stream evokes an involuntary emotional arousal of fear that precipitates a strong desire to flee.

Cognitive theorists adhere to a somewhat less essentialist view, allowing that emotional behavior remains an essentially physiological response to external stimuli but often mediated by processes of judgment and assessment or appraisal. In a sense, emotional expressions represent complex processes of neurophysiological arousal and cognitive processing that lead to certain conclusions about the meaning of certain stimuli within one's environment. It is the cognitive appraisal that allows us to conclude that despite being scared to death by an encounter with a mountain lion, the last thing we would want to do in that situation is run.

Others, however, claim that emotions are fundamentally social constructions and entirely dependent on the particular contexts in which they are manifest. From this point of view, emotions are "always experienced, understood and named via social and cultural processes" (Lupton, 1998, p. 15). Fear as an emotional response to the encounter of a mountain lion is therefore the result of a learned or acquired meaning schema. Learning to be very careful around hot stoves after having an unpleasant experience with one at an earlier point in one's life exemplifies this learned, constructed process.

Scholars representing this perspective are particularly interested in the implications that emotional experiences and expression hold for one's sense of self and one's relationships with others and the broader world. Lupton (1998) argues that within this group, positions reflect what she refers to as the "weak or less relativistic thesis" and the "strong thesis" (p. 15). While the former admits to a small range of emotions they consider naturally occurring and biologically given, the latter insists that emotion is, fundamentally and irreducibly, a "sociocultural product, wholly learnt and constructed through acculturation" (p. 15).

That is, the weak thesis might posit that we will naturally experience fear as a result of something like an encounter with a mountain lion, the consequence of the activities of the lower parts of our brain. But making sense of that fear within that particular situation is learned or acquired through one's social and cultural contexts. Proponents of the strong thesis would argue that one's emotional response to the encounter of a mountain lion in the depths of the forest is entirely the result of a set of meanings and relationships acquired over time within particular social and cultural contexts. As a child, we might have been read numerous fairy tales of similar creatures stalking unlikely innocents and making a quick lunch of them. These earlier experiences continued to be reinforced by similar myths and stories in popular culture of late adolescence and young adulthood. As an adult, the literal mountain lion might have morphed into more symbolic images, such as greedy corporations, heartless employers, and terrorists from other lands.

Emerging recently as a third major approach to understanding emotion is the idea of the emotional self as embodied, of recognizing, as Lupton (1998) suggests, the role that our flesh and blood play in emotion. But this perspective emphasizes more than just emotion as a bodily sensation. Rather, "embodiment is integral to, and inextricable from, subjectivity" (p. 32). From this viewpoint, emotion represents both the experience of particular body states and our interpretation or construction of these states as mediated by sociocultural processes.

For example, I might be in a curriculum meeting with colleagues in which we are reviewing proposed revisions in our graduate program. The meeting seems to be going well, but I gradually become aware of tightness in the back of my neck and shoulders. I might initially shrug it off as the product of my posture or the chair in which I am sitting, and I shift my weight and position. As the meeting proceeds, however, I notice that the tightness has become more, rather than less, pronounced. At the same time, I become aware of feeling vaguely uncertain about what is going on in the meeting, and the good feeling about the meeting I had earlier now evaporates. Before I know it, we seem to have two factions arguing heatedly about what seem to me quite obscure and innocuous points of the proposed curriculum plan. I recognize and interpret this tightness and discomfort in my body as a manifestation of anxiety. My experience of this emotion is the result of both attending to a physical sensation and framing this sensation within a broader discourse that leads to my naming it and experiencing it as anxiety.

Within the educational literature, the notion of embodied emotion is part of a broader conversation on embodied learning or knowing (Horn and Wilburn, 2005). According to Merriam, Caffarella, and Baumgartner (2007), "Embodied learning has a strong emotional or feeling dimension" (p. 194). It represents a theory of knowledge production that "depends on being in a world that is inseparable from our bodies, our language, and our social history" (Varela, Thompson, and Rosch, 1991, p. 149). Embodied learning represents a more holistic way of understanding learning and knowing (Barlas, 2001; Merriam, Caffarella, and Baumgartner, 2007) and is reflected in the work of scholars in adult and continuing education as well (Brooks and Clark, 2001; Chapman, 1998; Clark, 2001; Schlatner, 1994). Central to these views of embodied learning and knowing is the idea of the experience of emotion as embodied.

Variations of one or more of these three perspectives are evident in the growing discourse on emotion and adult learning (Jarvis, 2006; Merriam, Caffarella, and Baumgartner, 2007). In general, this discourse reflects an understanding of emotion as a neurophysiological response to an external or internal stimulus, occurring within and rendered meaningful through a particular sociocultural context and discourse, and integral to one's sense of self.

The Role of Emotion in Human Experience

Reflecting the influence of Cartesian dualism of mind and body and the growth of modernity, emotion has for many years been regarded as separate from both our cognitive and bodily processes, and an anathema to reason and knowing. Over the past twenty years, however, more holistic conceptions of the emotional self have become increasingly common. This holistic understanding of the emotional self implicates our emotions in an active process of knowing, suggesting a positive and "intelligent" role for them in our lives and, in particular, in adult learning.

Goleman's writing (1995) on the idea of emotional intelligence contributed significantly to a popular revision of the role of emotion in our private and social worlds. He suggests that human learning is constituted by both rational and emotional ways of knowing, but both are deeply integrated and bound up with one another. Emotional intelligence reflects self-awareness of one's own feelings and emotions, as well as those of others.

Emotional intelligence conveys the idea of emotions as something to be managed and used in our encounters with the outer world. Other scholars, however, attribute to emotion a more intrinsic intelligence, a way of knowing that augments or works in coordination with more traditional means of reason and cognition. In particular, feminist theory has been a major force in re-visioning our understanding of the role of emotions in our lives, rejecting the view of emotions as an obstacle to reason and knowledge, and helping to shape a deeper understanding of the role of emotions in the development of moral knowledge (Gorton, 2007). This re-visioning process has occurred largely within the broader focus of embodied knowing and learning (Merriam, Caffarella, and Baumgartner, 2007) and reflects conceptions of embodied emotion (Lupton, 1998).

Martha Nusbaum (2001) argues that emotions are characterized by a certain kind of intelligence and help us discern and make our way through our worlds. She rejects the widely popular image, carried over from the enlightenment, and its mind-body dualism, that emotions represent alien forces that invade and disrupt conscious, rational thought. Solomon (2007), who has explored and written about the emotions for many years, consistently links emotions to meaning in our lives. Similar to Nusbaum, Solomon rejects the idea of emotions as something happening to us or that they are, in a literal sense, irrational. Rather, he argues, emotions are intimately bound up with judgments we make, and they represent strategies for living these judgments within the world. "We live our lives through emotions," Solomon (2007) writes, "and it is our emotions that give our lives meaning" (p. 1).

Post-Jungians also emphasize the important role that emotions play in rendering meaning to our lives. While Solomon and Nusbaum represent a group of scholars that accord emotions an integral role in our rational understandings of the world, post-Jungian scholars such as Hillman (1975) and Watkins (2000) stress the importance of emotions to imaginative engagement with the world. Essentially, they argue, we can know ourselves and the world meaningfully only through the images that we create. These images are intimately bound up with our emotional experiences of the world. For these scholars, emotions represent expressions and ways of coming to know one's unconscious self, the fundamental source of meaning and creativity in our lives.

Emotion and Alternative Ways of Knowing in Adult Learning

Constructive and holistic approaches to emotion in adult learning represent what we may essentially consider as ways of knowing that challenge historical dominance of reason and scientific ways of knowing. These alternate ways of knowing are evident in theories of experiential learning, whole person learning, embodied learning, transformative learning, and spiritual experience. Emotional dimensions of our experiences represent central themes in theories of experiential learning. In particular, several authors (Boud, Keogh, and Walker, 1985; Boud and Miller, 1996; Beard and Wilson, 2002) provide suggestions for helping adult learners work through some of the emotions and feelings arising within their learning contexts.

Relying on the work of Heron (1992), Yorks and Kasl (2002) propose a phenomenological perspective to experiential learning. In this view, experience is regarded as "a process, an encounter with the world" (p. 182). Their theory of whole person learning posits a more holistic understanding of learning through experience and the foundational role of affect in this process (Yorks and Kasl, 2006).

Embodied learning suggests a way of experiential knowing that "depends on being in a world that is inseparable from our bodies, our language and our social history" (Varela, Thompson, and Rosch, 1991, p. 149). This approach stresses the importance of somatic awareness and recognizes the body as a source of knowledge about one's self and one's relationship to the world. Embodied learning is characterized by a strong emotional or feeling dimension (Merriam, Caffarella, and Baumgartner, 2007). Emotions convey a deep and intimate connection with our world, and this connection is often manifest neurophysiologically through the body.

Transformative learning theories incorporate aspects of experiential, whole person, and embodied learning. Although we lack consensus on a clear definition of transformative learning, most would agree that it represents a fundamental change or shift in our understanding of ourselves or our relationship with the world in which we live (Boyd and Myers, 1988; Cranton, 2006; Mezirow and Associates, 2000; O'Sullivan, 1999). Prompted by what is widely perceived as the rational and cognitive emphasis in Mezirow's (1991) theory of transformative learning (Cranton, 2006; Merriam, Caffarella, and Baumgartner, 2007), numerous scholars have been exploring the emotional or affective processes involved in transformative learning. In particular, Boyd and his colleagues (Boyd, 1991; Boyd and Myers, 1988; Dirkx, 2001, 2006) argue for the centrality of emotional processes in the expansion of consciousness and integration of personality, key dynamics of their view of transformative learning. Yorks and Kasl (2006) provide guidelines on how expressive ways of knowing can foster the growing awareness of emotion and emergence of transformative learning.

Finally, growing attention to spirituality in adult and higher education (English, Fenwick, and Parsons, 2003; Kazanjian and Laurence, 2002; Tisdell, 2003) also demonstrates a re-visioning of the role of emotions in human experience and learning, and stresses alternative ways of knowing (Palmer, 1993). Here, again, no consensus exists on a definition of spirituality. In general, however, a deep and abiding search for meaning is often associated with a process of developing or making explicit a connection with something greater than one's self, to community, a transcendent energy, or a divinity (English, Fenwick, and Parsons, 2003). Palmer (1993) argues that a sensitivity to feelings is essential to fostering the kind of spiritual journey that he believes education can or should represent. In contrast to our common practice of evading, suppressing, or otherwise not attending to feelings in teaching and learning, Palmer encourages us to create space within our educational environments where giving voice to emotion-laden issues becomes an integral part of a community of truth.

Conclusion

In the following chapters, the authors explore ways in which emotion is manifest in a variety of contexts of adult learning. These discussions offer a vision for integrating emotion within alternative ways of knowing in adult and higher education. They include programs for academically underprepared adults, adult learners returning to higher education, multicultural education, online education programs, workplace learning, nonformal learning, and the role of the arts in adult learning. From the perspectives of these various practice contexts, contributors explore a deeper understanding of the role that emotions play in contributing to and expressing one's sense of self as practitioner and as learner. The authors provide a consideration of key theoretical perspectives on how emotion constitutes our subjectivity or sense of self as adult learners and practitioners, and the various ways in which the emotional self is manifest within several different contexts of adult learning. Contributors discuss methods and strategies within various contexts that may be used to help practitioners and learners make sense of potentially powerful emotions evoked within the learning experience and how these experiences can help learners develop a deeper understanding of themselves.

New Directions for Adult and Continuing Education • DOI: 10.1002/ace

References

Barlas, C. "Learning-Within-Relationship as Context and Process in Adult Education." In R. O. Smith and others (eds.), *Forty-Second Annual Adult Education Research Conference and Proceedings*. East Lansing: Michigan State University, 2001.

Beard, C., and Wilson, J. P. *The Power of Experiential Learning: A Handbook for Educators and Trainers*. London: Kogan Page, 2002.

Boud, D., Keogh, R., and Walker, D. *Reflection: Turning Experiences into Learning.* London: Kogan Page, 1985.

Boud, D., and Miller, N. *Working with Experience: Animating Learning*. London: Routledge, 1996.

Boyd, R. D. *Personal Transformation in Small Groups: A Jungian Perspective*. New York: Routledge, 1991.

Boyd, R. D., and Myers, J. G. "Transformative Education." *International Journal of Lifelong Education,* 1988, 7(4), 261–284.

Brookfield, S. *Understanding and Facilitating Adult Learning*. San Francisco: Jossey-Bass, 1986.

Brooks, A., and Clark, C. "Narrative Dimensions of Transformative Learning." In R. O. Smith and others (eds.), *Forty-Second Annual Adult Education Research Conference and Proceedings*. East Lansing: Michigan State University, 2001.

Chapman, V. L. "Adult Education and the Body: Changing Performances of Teaching and Learning." In J. C. Kimmel (ed.), *Thirty-Ninth Annual Adult Education Conference Proceedings*. San Antonio: University of the Incarnate Word and Texas A&M, 1998.

Clark, M. C. "Off the Beaten Path: Some Creative Approaches to Adult Learning." In S. B. Merriam (ed.), *The New Update on Adult Learning Theory*. New Directions for Adult and Continuing Education, no. 89. San Francisco: Jossey-Bass, 2001.

Cranton, P. *Understanding and Promoting Transformative Learning: A Guide for Educators of Adults*. San Francisco: Jossey-Bass, 2006.

Dirkx, J. M. "The Power of Feelings: Emotion, Imagination, and the Construction of Meaning in Adult Learning." In S. B. Merriam (ed.), *The New Update on Adult Learning Theory*. New Directions for Adult and Continuing Education, no. 89. San Francisco: Jossey-Bass, 2001.

Dirkx, J. M. "Engaging Emotions in Adult Learning: A Jungian Perspective on Emotion and Transformative Learning." In E. Taylor (ed.), *Fostering Transformative Learning in the Classroom: Challenges and Innovations*. New Directions in Adult and Continuing Education, no. 109. San Francisco: Jossey-Bass, 2006.

Dirkx, J. M., and Spurgin, M. "Implicit Theories of Adult Basic Education Teachers: How They Think About Their Students." *Adult Basic Education: An Interdisciplinary Journal for Adult Literacy Educators,* 1992, 2, 20–41.

English, L. M., Fenwick, T. J., and Parsons, J. *Spirituality of Adult Education and Training*. Malabar, Fla.: Krieger, 2003.

Goleman, D. *Emotional Intelligence: Why It Can Matter More Than IQ*. New York: Bantam Books, 1995.

Gorton, K. "Theorizing Emotion and Affect." *Feminist Theory,* 2007, 8(3), 333–348.

Heron, J. *Feeling and Personhood: Psychology in Another Key*. Thousand Oaks, Calif.: Sage, 1992.

Hillman, J. *Re-Visioning Psychology.* New York: HarperCollins, 1975.

Horn, J., and Wilburn, D. "The Embodiment of Learning." *Educational Philosophy and Theory,* 2005, 37(5), 745–760.

Jarvis, P. *Toward a Comprehensive Theory of Human Learning*. London: Routledge, 2006.

Jones, R. M. *Fantasy and Feeling in Education*. New York: HarperCollins, 1968.

Kazanjian, V. H., and Laurence, P. L. (eds.). *Education as Transformation: Religious Pluralism, Spirituality, and a New Vision for Higher Education in America*. New York: Peter Lang, 2002.

Lewis, M., and Haviland-Jones, J. M. (eds). *Handbook of Emotions*. (2nd ed.) New York: Guilford Press, 2000.

Lindeman, E. C. *The Meaning of Adult Education*. New York: New Republic, 1926.

Lupton, D. *The Emotional Self: A Sociocultural Exploration*. Thousand Oaks, Calif.: Sage, 1998.

Merriam, S. B., Caffarella, R. S., and Baumgartner, L. M., *Learning in Adulthood: A Comprehensive Guide*. San Francisco: Jossey-Bass, 2007.

Mezirow, J. *Transformative Dimensions of Adult Learning*. San Francisco: Jossey-Bass, 1991.

Mezirow, J., and Associates. *Learning as Transformation: Critical Perspectives on a Theory in Progress*. San Francisco: Jossey-Bass, 2000.

Nusbaum, M. *Upheavals of Thought: The Intelligence of Emotions*. Cambridge: Cambridge University Press, 2001.

O'Sullivan, E. *Transformative Learning: Educational Vision for the 21st Century*. London: Zed, 1999.

Palmer, P. *To Know as We Are Known: Education as a Spiritual Journey*. New York: HarperSanFrancisco, 1993.

Rogers, C. R. *Freedom to Learn*. Columbus, Ohio: Charles E. Merrill, 1969.

Salzberger-Wittenberg, I., Henry, G., and Osborne, E. *The Emotional Experience of Teaching and Learning*. London: Routledge and Kegan Paul, 1983.

Schlatner, C. "The Body in Transformative Learning." In M. Hymans, J. Armstrong, and E. Anderson (eds.), *Thirty-Fifth Annual Adult Education Research Conference Proceedings*. Knoxville, Tenn.: University of Knoxville, 1994.

Schutz, P. A., Hong, J. Y., Cross, D. I., and Osbon, J. N. "Reflections on Investigating Emotion in Educational Activity Settings." *Educational Psychology Review*, 2006, *18*, 343–360.

Solomon, R. C. *True to Our Feelings: What Emotions Are Really Telling Us*. New York: Oxford University Press, 2007.

Tisdell, E. J. *Exploring Spirituality and Culture in Adult and Higher Education*. San Francisco: Jossey-Bass, 2003.

Varela, F., Thompson, E., & Rosch, E. *The Embodied Mind: Cognitive Science and Human Experience*. Cambridge, Mass.: MIT Press, 1991.

Watkins, M. *Invisible Guests: The Development of Imaginal Dialogues*. Woodstock, Conn.: Spring, 2000.

Yorks, L., and Kasl, E. "Toward a Theory and Practice for Whole-Person Learning: Reconceptualizing Experience and the Role of Affect." *Adult Education Quarterly*, 2002, *52*, 176–192.

Yorks, L., and Kasl, E. "I Know More Than I Can Say: A Taxonomy for Using Expressive Ways of Knowing to Foster Transformative Learning." *Journal of Transformative Education*, 2006, *4*(1), 43–64.

JOHN M. DIRKX is professor of higher, adult, and lifelong education at Michigan State University.

2

This chapter considers strengths-based approaches to supporting learning for adults facing challenges in their abilities to engage in and commit to adult learning programs, and offers directions for policy and practice.

Adults in Programs for the "Academically Underprepared"

Janet Isserlis

Adult basic education represents a marginalized field that addresses the needs of a largely marginalized population: adults who are viewed through a deficit lens labeling them as being underprepared. Some speak the language of the country in which they were born. (For purposes of this chapter, I examine learners and learning in English-speaking countries.) Having been pushed out of high school in the wake of high-stakes testing or having been socially promoted, many have been handed a high school diploma while lacking the ability to use print to access information, as a vehicle of expression, as a tool for accomplishing tasks in the world, and as a means of gaining control, connection, and meaning.

Other adult learners are immigrants to English-speaking countries in need of language and literacy development in their first language or in English, and they are viewed warily in some quarters, particularly since the attacks on September 11, 2001. The circumstances of their immigration vary and include professionals from one country wielding mops in their new country, refugees escaping war and upheaval, and "economic" immigrants, needing to earn enough money to support families or return to their countries of origin. In almost every case, adult learners are perceived as being less than—that is, in need of remediation, employment skills, and language and literacy development. Many lack the needed documentation to vote or participate through official channels in the lives of their communities.

Government policies, however, define approaches to addressing the needs of these learners in an increasingly narrow manner. In outlining

NEW DIRECTIONS FOR ADULT AND CONTINUING EDUCATION, no. 120, Winter 2008 © 2008 Wiley Periodicals, Inc.
Published online in Wiley InterScience (www.interscience.wiley.com) • DOI: 10.1002/ace.312

federal funding parameters, the Division of Adult Education and Literacy within the U.S. Department of Education describes adult education programs as those "that help American adults get the basic skills they need to be productive workers, family members, and citizens. . . . These programs emphasize basic skills such as reading, writing, math, English language competency, and problem-solving" (U.S. Department of Education, n.d.). In applying the principles of No Child Left Behind to adult education programs, the U.S. Department of Education (2005) emphasizes an accountability system, requiring providers to measure learning through standardized assessments, account for improving the literacy skills of participants, and improve classroom instruction.

Given these increasingly narrow constraints, it is not surprising that adult learners find it challenging to enter into, learn within, and complete adult education courses. Programs are challenged to recruit, reward, and retain students and personnel in a field funded by an office that prides itself on accountability, while failing to offer official recognition of progress beyond that measured by standardized instruments.

This chapter examines particular challenges and strengths of adult learners in basic education programs (including literacy, English language, and adult secondary preparation), the affective issues that have bearing on their relative ability to be present to learning, and the ways in which adult educators at program and policy levels might address these challenges in order to make adult learning more productive and useful for all concerned.

What It Looks Like

One adult education student misses class because she cannot leave her children alone at home. Another student arrives late because a partner promised to give her a ride, only to undermine her by stopping first for gas and then for coffee. A third student is in her seat, notebook open, pen in hand, but she is unable to make sense of the letters and words written on the blackboard. Within the class, a person is writing and another waiting for the teacher to help him at his seat.

Adult educators likely recognize these learners and their responses to emotional, physical, or sexual abuse or to the ordinary stressors present in the seemingly simple process of leaving home or work to get to school. We may also recognize aspects of these scenarios and responses within our own lives. While this chapter focuses on learners and learning in adult basic education contexts, it is critical to note that violence and trauma affect many adults in many different contexts. While we consider how to support learning for those enrolled in adult education programs, we must also keep in mind that histories of trauma may be present in the lives of teachers, administrators, adult students, and many others, and they cut across race, class, ethnic, and professional boundaries.

New Directions for Adult and Continuing Education • DOI: 10.1002/ace

The learning contexts described here involve adults who, largely because of some form of disruption in their lives, seek to increase their basic skills and abilities, often with a goal of new or better employment possibilities. Sometimes they choose to participate, but at times they are required to attend as a condition of receipt of public assistance or an order by a court or other agency. Many learners return to educational settings with hesitation: "Having 'failed' at school a first time, finding the confidence to try it again poses significant challenges, and often causes intense anxiety for learners before even entering the adult classroom. For adults who have had experiences of violence, have been told by abusers that they're stupid, these anxieties and self-doubts can be overwhelming" (Isserlis, 2001, p. 4). Students attend classes sporadically, show up late, leave early, and appear to be inattentive. Horsman's early work (1990) with women in rural Nova Scotia sparked a process of problematizing and challenging educators' perception of problems focused on students' behavior, attendance patterns, learning styles, and abilities. She named and called into question mainstream teachers' responses to so-called problems such as referring to inconsistent attendance as a *lack of motivation,* incomplete homework assignments as indicative of *laziness,* a lack of participation in classes as demonstrating a *lack of interest or daydreaming,* and reticence to speak as reflective of *inattentiveness* (Isserlis, 2001).

Horsman (1999) and others have begun to name the fact that adult learners live complicated lives, bring complicated experience bases with them to learning contexts, and may be more or less present to and ready for learning than educators had widely understood. The complexity of these learners' lives often masks the critical strategies they develop to cope and get through the day—strategies that practitioners often overlook or simply do not see. Many, though not all, adult education practitioners have done well in traditional schooling, seldom experiencing hesitation in classes, answering questions with confidence, and participating enthusiastically in group discussions. Like other forms of unearned privilege, such as race or class, school itself can privilege those for whom literacy acquisition comes easily. For those for whom learning did not come so readily, school represents a location in which to develop strategies to become invisible, gain positive attention through negative behavior, tolerate, or simply get through the day. In adjusting to new systems and expectations, immigrant and refugee learners attempting to master English language literacy and spoken communication face parallel hurdles.

Many adult learners also bring histories of violence and upheaval to the classroom. Their responses to these experiences have led them to develop coping strategies that range from "an all or nothing approach to learning and relationships, a lack of presence, living in crisis mode, issues with trust and boundaries and silences and disclosures" (Morrish, Horsman, and Hofer, 2002, p. 15). Other adults, even those whose lives have been less fraught or who have experienced little success in or control over prior encounters with formal education, respond in a similar wary way to a return to school.

Recognizing that this first step of entering into a program can be treacherous for many, educators have begun to focus on orientation processes to welcome learners to their programs. (This emphasis reflects the influence of work in studies) of learner persistence by Comings and his colleagues (Comings, 2007). This body of work identifies ways in which adults stop in and out of classes, reasons they are likely to stay, and ways to identify and address their needs from the first encounter (Malicky, Katz, Norton, and Norman, 1997). In an effort to assist learners in planning their education and to help with data tracking and accountability, many state offices of adult education now require explicit policies delineating orientation and goal-setting processes.

At best, these processes, along with the requisite support and professional development, can aid practitioners in finding ways to engage learners at their points of readiness. But they run the risk of becoming little more than lists of component elements to be checked off, indicating that a student has been through some intake and goal-setting process. Furthermore, the officially sanctioned or measurable goals that count toward marking learner and program progress are limited to pursuing training beyond adult basic education, obtaining or retaining employment, or earning a high school credential. In emphasizing this form of learner achievement, these processes often fail to recognize smaller and more meaningful goals, such as learning to read a chapter book, spending more time reading with one's children, or keeping a journal. For learners who are underprepared, achievement of these smaller goals is critical to the achievement of the larger ones. Programs are sometimes forced, then, to accept those students most likely to achieve the official goals, effectively creaming the adult learner population in order to achieve mandated outcomes.

In order to strengthen programs' abilities to welcome and work with underprepared learners, practitioners need to realize both the strengths and fears adults who lack school privilege may experience. The following message, posted by John Ward (n.d.) to the Adult Literacy Professional Development Discussion List, reflects the pervasive nature of fear that many adults experience when encountering new challenges and trying something new:

> I would like to respond to why people needing help in reading don't attend school. One major reason is fear. Fear that people in the school will not understand why you're so much different than they are. There are the disabilities of learning how to read. I also feel the way that some people are brought up. As . . . a young person living with two parents that were alcoholics, my dad worked, my mum was never around, always in a bar room. Trying to raise four brothers and two sisters when I was 8 and 9 years old. My younger siblings were more important to me than school at that time. Also,

New Directions for Adult and Continuing Education • DOI: 10.1002/ace

always fearing when the cops came knocking at the door, knowing that they were here to take us away from our parents and that it was my responsibility to hide and protect them from the cops. As I grew up and winging it with a sense that I didn't really need the help until I was involved in an accident that took a life. At that time I also didn't really have anything to live for. . . . I went to vocational rehab, and she gave me the idea to go back to school. It gave me reasons to live and to show my sons that their father could accomplish something by putting his mind to it. . . . I suggest you work with vocational rehab people to get those people who are ready for a change in their life in the door of the classroom. I also think you should allow people into the classroom to come to visit to check out how adult education works. It doesn't mean you have to join, but to see if you would feel comfortable there. Make sure the learning time is welcoming and can get the fear to go away.

Many of us do not like to fail; some fear success. The characteristics of adult learners described in this chapter reflect traits common to many adults, regardless of educational status, but for these learners, these characteristics influence their abilities to learn and thrive within educational settings.

What We Can Do About It

That practitioners must find ways to engage adults in learning regardless of their relative ability to be present to learning is clear. By *present*, I mean an ability to attend to learning, to focus and engage. Recognizing an adult's all-or-nothing view of learning means understanding that the student who enters in the fall, hoping to earn a general educational development diploma by winter, may be set up to fail for two major reasons. First, if adults are not learning English or preparing for specific employment sectors, the diploma seems to be the only end point, the only nameable goal in adult basic education. Second, and more germane to this discussion, those who have experienced systemic violence, including poverty, racism, and a range of disabilities leading to multiple incidents of failure at school, may need assistance in finding a middle ground, identifying and negotiating small steps to achieving goals, and, especially, understanding that one or even several errors along the way do not mean that nothing can be learned or that the learner is stupid. Instead, adults need specific feedback such as praise that recognizes real progress and transparency in addressing errors. Learners need to see their own progress and understand how mistakes can further learning. Many of us see errors as signs of failure, not as indicators of learning processes. For example, practitioners can help a learner see why reading *brother* for *bother* indicates that she is beginning to recognize the word, and now she needs to know how to read carefully. Practitioners can let the learner know that stopping when *brother* makes no sense in the sentence, "It doesn't brother me," is a smart mistake, because she is reading for

New Directions for Adult and Continuing Education • DOI: 10.1002/ace

meaning, bringing her prior knowledge to the task. She needs to understand that good readers stop when something does not make sense and start over again.

The work goes on in a processive manner. Practitioners viewing learning and learners through a strengths-based lens can recognize learners' needs in relation to their strengths. Building trust and community within small groups and one-on-one tutoring means enabling learners to choose to share information as best suits their needs. Some learners expend a great deal of energy deciding what to tell to whom and what to keep secret. For some learners, this leaves little room to attend to learning. In classrooms, practitioners can establish a basic ground rule with learners: anyone can ask anyone anything, and anyone can say when they do not want to answer a particular question. This ground rule may be a way to give permission to everyone to exert control over the information they offer to the group.

Framing writing assignments and language activities that require learners to disclose information about their own lives can be damaging to the learning process. Practitioners can use strategies, such as responding to a prompt about "something I like," that allow learners to respond with as much or as little personal information as they choose. By doing so, they let learners know that they can as easily talk about a movie they like as they can about their family or childhood. Educators are not counselors, but they must be attentive listeners. Understanding the likelihood of adults' having experienced difficulties means accepting and embracing the possibilities of multiple modes of learning, of supporting learning through taking time and thoughtfully making progress clear to the learner.

The discourse of medicalizing adults' problems is one that manages only to set them up for increased failure within mainstream educational programs. For example, telling a student not to come to school if she has not addressed her issues, to solve her problem, and then she will be welcomed back to school communicates to a learner that she cannot even try to attend classes until she is "better." Lewis (1999) debunks the myth of "curing" trauma and recognizes that not all survivors of trauma can be "good victims" by "getting over" their experiences and getting on with their lives. Instead, Lewis suggests that memories and damage caused by trauma never really go away for many people. Some students can learn to live beside the trauma and understand that it may come and go. This realization opens the possibility of moving forward while acknowledging that although difficult moments can and will arise, they do not have to be the defining way in which survivors might develop ongoing coping strategies. Lewis's assertion moves us beyond the discourse of victim and recognizes that identity is not determined solely by traumatic events.

At times, a learner may need to leave a program to address a critical problem, but often he or she is dealing with chronic issues alongside participation in a learning program. Instead of perpetuating a cycle through which an adult believes she may never be prepared to learn, practitioners

New Directions for Adult and Continuing Education • DOI: 10.1002/ace

can use an approach that helps learners acknowledge challenges while also realistically naming what they can do in classrooms. Such an approach will assist adults with the difficult challenge of reentering formal learning.

Increasingly, community-based adult learning programs are taking trauma and histories of upheaval into account in planning instruction and program design, and they are finding ways to change policy and practice to accommodate learners' needs and abilities. Examples include flexible attendance policies, learner support or leadership groups, and case management support or referral systems. Ongoing professional development programs can enable all practitioners, including teachers, staff, volunteers, and administrators, to understand and appropriately respond to impacts of difficulties in learners' lives as part of an ongoing process of creating safer, more viable spaces for learning.

Learners and practitioners need to deconstruct notions of success and failure and to problematize notions of self-esteem so we are able to acknowledge how ignoring our own school privilege gets in the way of understanding the perspectives and self-images of many learners. This confidence or fearlessness in taking risks in school has been so normalized as to be invisible to many practitioners and policymakers. Practitioners who can see where their own self-confidence is similar to and different from those of their learners may gain insight into ways of productively engaging learners in the project of learning through understanding where learning is scary, intimidating, and difficult. They can then also work with learners to find places where learning can occur with fewer obstacles, where taking a little more time might be the only thing keeping someone back, where encouraging students to help one another might be one of many useful ways of helping them take control of, and pleasure in, their learning over time.

Finally, in order to support adult learning and to further adults' chances of participating fully and successfully in their learning, teachers, administrators, and funders need to understand the complex process of learning and the support required to ensure it occurs, and to call for needed shifts in practice and policy. Professional development must incorporate a focus on the impact of affective elements of learning on ongoing materials and curriculum development, and they must inform training in instructional methodology and teaching strategies. Adult learners themselves are among the most valuable resources for learning more about learning. We need to listen to them attentively.

References

Comings, J. "Persistence: Helping Adult Education Students Reach Their Goals." *Review of Adult Learning and Literacy*, 7, 2007. Retrieved Dec. 27, 2007, from http://www. ncsall.net/index.php?id=1175.

Horsman, J. *Something in My Mind Besides the Everyday: Women and Literacy.* Toronto: Women's Press, 1990.

Horsman, J. *Too Scared to Learn: Women, Violence, and Education.* Toronto: McGilligan Books, 1999.

Isserlis, J. *On the Screen: Bringing Women's Barriers to Literacy, Learning and Employment to Light.* Washington, D.C.: National Institute for Literacy, 2001. Retrieved Dec. 26, 2007, from http://www.brown.edu/Departments/Swearer_Center/Literacy_Resources/1Writings.pdf.

Lewis, T. *Living Beside: Performing Normal After Incest Memories Return.* Toronto: McGilligan Books, 1999.

Malicky, G. V., Katz, C. H., Norton, M., & Norman, C. A. "Literacy Learning in a Community-Based Program." *Adult Basic Education,* 1997, 7(2), 84–103.

Morrish, E., Horsman, J., and Hofer, J. *Take on the Challenge: A Source Book from the Women, Violence, and Adult Education Project.* Boston: World Education, 2002.

U.S. Department of Education. "Helping Adults Become Literate." 2005. Retrieved Aug. 14, 2007, from http://www.ed.gov/nclb/methods/reading/adultliteracy.html.

U.S. Department of Education. "Adult Education and Literacy." N.d. Retrieved Aug. 14, 2007, from http://www.ed.gov/about/offices/list/ovae/pi/AdultEd/index.html.

Ward, J. "Re: Hard to Reach People with Low Literacy Skills." Message posted to National Institute for Literacy Professional Development 776. Retrieved Aug. 3, 2007, from http://www.nifl.gov/pipermail/professionaldevelopment/2007/000778.html.

JANET ISSERLIS is a literacy specialist at the Rhode Island Adult Education Professional Development Center and also works with adult education and prison-based programs through the Howard R. Swearer Center for Public Service at Brown University.

3

Through acts of hope, adults face four challenges of emotion in their pursuits of collegiate learning.

Emotional Challenges of Adult Learners in Higher Education

Carol E. Kasworm

Learning is an act of hope. Although adults enter learning experiences from many frames of emotion and cognitive beliefs, each views this experience as the purposeful choice for a new and different future, a future of hope and possibilities. Thus, as Taylor (2006) suggested, quoting from the Talmud, "We do not see things as they are, we see them as we are" (p. 200). For adult learners, the pursuit of higher education is a choice and a life-changing engagement.

Given the courage and the fragility of adult students, this chapter explores four key emotional challenges of the complex journey in developing a successful student identity. The premise for this exploration is that adult students live in multiple worlds: worlds of action and commitment, worlds of emotional validation and conflict, and worlds that will change both the mind and the heart.

Entering College to Succeed

Adults, unlike younger adult collegiate learners, do not view themselves as typically going away to college, as starting a separated life from family and community. Whether they sometimes are pushed into collegiate learning through losing a job or voluntarily seek out college to develop a different life opportunity, college for most adults is not a physical separation from their past worlds. Rather, most adults continue their complex lives—with the added challenging role of student. Many of these adult students are

NEW DIRECTIONS FOR ADULT AND CONTINUING EDUCATION, no. 120, Winter 2008 © 2008 Wiley Periodicals, Inc.
Published online in Wiley InterScience (www.interscience.wiley.com) • DOI: 10.1002/ace.313

continuing a previously interrupted journey of college studies, a journey that expands their world of commitments and possibilities. Another subgroup of adults enters college as a new, unknown journey. They seek out college for the first time to either reinvent themselves through a new environment of people and ideas or to build a life with possibilities to support a more stable future. Whether these adults are expanding their lives, investing in a new career option, or reinventing themselves, entry is often a complex and treacherous journey that supports but may also diminish their sense of identity.

The first act of hope for adult learners is seeking entry to college. Confident and resilient learners find entry into college often challenging to their identities and their sense of adult competence. Although these individuals typically have a sense of mission and purpose and often a long-term plan for their collegiate pursuits, they experience doubts and insecurity. They may face challenges negotiating the institutional procedures, the time commitments and demands of course work, and the ego demands of classroom assessment. They may sometimes be discouraged or disheartened. However, these individuals present attitudes, skills, and beliefs of resilience and risk taking; they believe that they have a high probability of success and are committed to quality learning experiences and a collegiate credential.

Of greater concern for adult educators are adult students who often are unsure of themselves and their futures, whether they are first-time-entry or reentry students. They often seek college entry through a life crisis, such as divorce or separation, work issues, or some form of significant individual need, such as seeking a career with financial stability. These adults display emotional chaos as they develop a student identity, contemplate future success in a collegiate classroom, and psychologically manage their turbulent life circumstances. In addition, they may have unresolved life issues that draw on their energy and time, as well as potentially negative past experiences of learning that create additional anxiety. They often have a questioning sense of who they are, what they should be doing as learners, and how they can be effective and successful in a collegiate environment. Furthermore, these adults may have fragile financial support and equally fragile interpersonal supports to pursue a college degree.

Given these emotional conditions, one of the first acts of hope for the adult entering higher education is to purposefully decide to be a college student. These individuals need the courage and support to apply for admission, register for classes, and participate in collegiate courses. Drawing on their past life experiences and their evaluation of their past learning, these individuals enter the classroom with an evolving and sometimes conflicted learner identity. Research suggests that many adult learners experience significant anxiety and self-consciousness about their acceptance, place in a collegiate environment, and ability to perform as undergraduate students (Kasworm, 2005, 2006). They often experience issues with family, coworkers, and key friends who are not supportive of this new involvement and its

New Directions for Adult and Continuing Education • DOI: 10.1002/ace

demands. Although each adult uniquely experiences these potentially tense beginnings, their anxieties often dissipate after successful entry and completion of several courses. Through their engagement and adaptation to the role and rigors of student life, these individuals usually develop a sense of their place in a college environment, a voice for student learning, and the belief of personal success in this academic context. Their initial entry is buoyed with special positive validation from other older students and faculty, as well as friendship and assistance from select younger students and collegiate staff (Kasworm, 2005). Furthermore, many adults have reported that their children, their spouse, their siblings, and sometimes their coworkers provide initial support and encouragement for this long journey.

What provides the supportive collegiate bridge for these adults' emotional engagement into college studies? Key authorities highlight the importance of supportive messages in the collegiate literature of programs and services; key staff provide personal attention and advisement with admissions entry, career advisement, potential basic skills and study strategies courses and supports, and an institutional climate that welcomes adults into their programs (Kasworm, Polson, and Fishback, 2002). A number of institutions have stylized adult degree programs and adult student units that offer a special instructional environment, support services, and an adult-friendly culture. Many offer special offices to serve adults, as well as orientation programs directed to adults, first-year-cohort courses for adults, and adult student organizations. All of these structures and programs create responsive and supportive opportunities to aid the entry of adults.

Continuing in College Through Renegotiation or Adaptation

The second act of hope by adult students is their ongoing engagement in a collegiate environment. Because adults have competing lives, hopes, and realities, each semester of college involvement represents either a renegotiation or adaptation of themselves and their lives. Although there is historic contrary evidence, Calcagnoa, Crosta, Bailey, and Jenkins (2006a) noted in a recent major analysis (2006b) that adults were more likely to persist in college in comparison to younger adult students:

> Older students have a clearer sense of their objectives for going to college, they know how to navigate the educational bureaucracy, and they are generally not as shy about asking for help or demanding service. Older students are less easily discouraged or thrown off course, even though they often have more outside pressures and obligations than do younger students [2006a, pp. 23–24].

Part of this persistence and learning engagement is supported by the theory of socioemotional selectivity, which suggests that the perception of time that adult learners have plays a fundamental role regarding these emotional engagements in significant academic learning. When time is perceived as limited, emotion-related goals assume primacy. As Carstensen, Isaacowitz, and Charles (1999) suggest, "Older people relative to their younger counterparts describe their futures as limited and recognize that they do not have 'all the time in the world' left to pursue their goals" (p. 168). Thus, adults select challenging life goals "even at the cost of emotional satisfaction. . . . During this period of life, the exploration of the world demands emotional resilience in the face of failures and social rejections" (p. 168). This theory captures the paradoxical place of the adult student as an emotional self and a knowledge-striving self. The cognitive and the emotional aspects of their collegiate commitment are intertwined and represent both emotional resilience and emotional vulnerability. Thus, faculty and staff need to understand the paradoxical focus and goals of adult students. They need to have adult-supportive policies and instructional designs for adults experiencing this emotional learning journey.

Beyond the demands of limited time parameters to pursue college, adults also need to experience the connected classroom. Because of complex individual identities, adult students best learn through key acts of meaning making connected to their adult identities. The connected classroom represents this social and psychological space for learning, connecting the adult's life to academic studies and other key adult life roles (Kasworm, Polson, and Fishback, 2002). Because adult students continue with their complex adult lives, the classroom world should ideally connect them with their other worlds. In particular, the most powerful influences on adults are class-related learning successes and their relationships with faculty validating their adult identity as worthy and valued (Graham and Donaldson, 1999; Kasworm, Polson, and Fishback, 2002). In essence, adult students engage in higher education based in an emotionally connected place. This place, the connected classroom environment, provides the collegiate social context for learning and for defining their success as college students. This place validates their other sense of self as knowledgeable and competent adult actors, as well as potentially challenging their values, beliefs, and behaviors in these roles to imagine and perceive different possibilities and understandings. Although learning may sometimes be threatening and uncomfortable, the connected classroom provides the supportive ballast for adults to consider dissonant ideas and images of their world.

Becoming One in the World of Collegiate Learning

The third act of hope for adults focuses on their engagement in learning new knowledge, as well as new perspectives and potentially new beliefs. These adult students engage in learning through co-construction of meanings between their individual understandings, the knowledge and skills presented in the course and text, and the faculty and fellow students' understandings.

New Directions for Adult and Continuing Education • DOI: 10.1002/ace

These co-constructed meanings represent the adult life of the known and unknown, the cognitive and the affective. The paradox of this third act of hope is that adults are often taught to learn discipline content and skill yet engage in learning through their life experiences; they view the world through their past and current adult roles, not typically through the discipline perspective. As Pepin (1988) suggested, "We constantly attempt to create the world in our image, to contain it within structures we have available to us" (pp. 176–177). The challenge of higher education in serving adults is to create both learning that reflects the current adult learner's world and creates possible alternative understandings of that world in relation to the enhancement of critical thinking, multiple worldviews, and self-authorship.

In recent research, adult undergraduates were found to negotiate the meaning of their undergraduate learning in elaborate and complex patterns, characterized as meaning structures or knowledge voices (Kasworm, 2003). These patterns represented epistemological beliefs of the learner embedded in two worlds: the world of academic knowledge (of books and theory) and the world known by many adults as real-world knowledge (of tacit understandings and everyday applications). Beliefs and the utility of these two forms of knowledge influenced adult students' goals and eventual outcomes for learning. Furthermore, these meaning structures were not just cognitive lenses for engaging and retaining classroom knowledge. These knowledge voices also represented affective connections to self, life roles, and life actions.

In considering these knowledge voices, two of the voices represented adult undergraduate beliefs that collegiate learning should be anchored and reinforced through their practical world experiences and their current adult role identities (Kasworm, 2003). These two voices, the Outside voice and the Cynical voice, place affective and cognitive emphasis on knowledge that validates and reinforces current adult beliefs, roles, and related life action contexts. Adults operating from these two voices selectively engage in learning knowledge that does not contradict their understandings of how they see themselves and their worlds. If these students are required to memorize and be graded on knowledge that is contradictory to their beliefs, they will rely on learning through short-term memory recall and readily dismiss this knowledge beyond the requirements of the course.

Two other knowledge voices of adults present a belief of the two separate knowledge worlds, but with a primary anchor based in the academic world of knowledge. In the first pattern, Entry voice, adult students view themselves as novices in the stylized environment of the college classroom. Thus, they compartmentalize their prior understandings of self-efficacy and competence in their adult life worlds, believing that their backgrounds have limited or no value in the academic world. The second voice, the Straddling voice, represents a knowledge structure of students who delineate incoming knowledge and act on that knowledge through different worlds: the academic world of knowledge and the real world of knowledge. In this knowledge structure, these students operate with bifurcation of knowledge and related affective understandings; they learn and act on knowledge separately through the academic and the real worlds. The fifth and final pattern, the Inclusion voice, represents the integration of knowledge engagement across both life worlds. It demonstrates a unification of the cognitive and emotional worlds of adult students and their epistemological beliefs of different worlds of academic knowledge and knowledge based in adult life roles. In this knowledge structure, these students unify their understandings and beliefs through the broader conceptual thinking and decision making anchored in the intellectual understandings of the academy. They view both their real-world roles and their collegiate learning through multiple theoretical frames of understanding. Adults in this final voice often suggest actions of transformation of self through an ongoing active cycle of reflection and action integrating knowledge and life applications. For these adult students, the power of learning has an impact on both the life of the mind and of the self. As Mezirow and Associates (2000) suggested, through the process of transformational learning, adult students become different people, viewing themselves, their families, and their world from new and different perspectives.

These patterns of epistemological meaning making through knowledge voices highlight the importance of faculty respect and differentiated responsiveness to adult learners, as well as faculty skill in designing connected classrooms for both the intellectual and the emotional worlds of learning. As outlined more extensively in other discussions (Kasworm, 2003), faculty can provide invaluable support and appropriate intellectual challenges for adults in these varied epistemological states. Furthermore, adult students are not passive within these classrooms; they continually engage in metacognitive decision processes related to classroom engagement, identifying relevancy and importance of classroom knowledge in relation to themselves and their adult lives. Some choose to dismiss the content and the faculty member as irrelevant, while others attempt to create further understandings and applications through self-directed learning actions beyond the classroom.

Considering Future Possibilities

As the final act of hope, adult learners also face challenges in gaining a place, a position, a voice, and a related sense of valued self in the cultural worlds of higher education. Because the collegiate setting is significantly valued by society and is often a selective, discriminating learning world, adult learners also experience emotional cultural demands in relation to this setting. As expressed by adult learners' positional and relational identities (Holland, Lachicotte, Skinner, and Cain, 1998), adults actively negotiate their sense of place, social authority and agency, and relatedness to others who value or marginalize their presence. Although adults bring a rich and complex adult identity into the collegiate environment, they face unique challenges to their identity through the varied supportive and negative sociocultural contexts of higher education. Whether within the classroom or experiencing the broader social world of the college, they experience environmental and relational cues, messages, and supports (or lack thereof). These adults identify through these cultural cues which students matter and the valued student behaviors for success in this context. Through these cultural engagements, adults co-construct their sense of who they are as collegiate students (in relation to other students and in relation to their other adult roles) and their sense of possibilities to be successful and valued in both this academic world and many other adult worlds. They come to image themselves as actors in future learning possibilities or to resist future learning opportunities as identity threatening based on their current cultural experience. This last act of hope suggests that learning is not just within the adult; it is co-constructed through cultural and social interactions within a specific context that can unify or fracture the learner identity of the adult. Context does matter in the emotional journey of the learner.

Conclusion

Through these four acts of hope, adult learners experience the evolving development of a student identity. "We do not see things as they are, we see them as we are" (Taylor, 2006, p. 200). Adult students come as highly complex yet ever changing selves. They negotiate their sense of an adult student identity based in who they are and who they wish to become, as well as through the complex interactive environment of the collegiate world. Through acts of hope, they engage in a rich repertoire of emotional and cognitive needs while locating their place and voice in the classroom, of negotiating positional and relational agency in relation to their fellow students, faculty, staff, and the institution. At the heart of collegiate learning is the recognition of the adult as not just a mind at work, but also of a complex individual who is both a learner and a contributor to the class and the institution.

References

Calcagnoa, J., Crosta, P., Bailey, T., and Jenkins, D. "Does Age of Entrance Affect Community College Completion Probabilities? Evidence from a Discrete-Time Hazard Model." 2006a. Unpublished manuscript.

Calcagnoa, J., Crosta, P., Bailey, T., and Jenkins, D. "Stepping Stones to a Degree: The Impact of Enrollment Pathways and Milestones on Older Community College Student Outcomes." *CCCR Working Paper No. 4*, 2006b. Retrieved October 1, 2008, from http://ccrc.tc.columbia.edu/Publication.asp?uid=452.

Carstensen, L., Isaacowitz, D., and Charles, S. "Taking Time Seriously: A Theory of Socioemotional Selectivity." *American Psychologist*, 1999, *54(3)*, 165–181.

Graham, S., and Donaldson, J. S. "Adult Students' Academic and Intellectual Development in College." *Adult Education Quarterly,* 1999, *49*(3), 147–161.

Holland, D., Lachicotte, W. J., Skinner, D., and Cain, C. *Identity and Agency in Cultural Worlds.* Cambridge, Mass.: Harvard University Press, 1998.

Kasworm, C. "Adult Meaning Making in the Undergraduate Classroom." *Adult Education Quarterly,* 2003, *53*(2), 81–98.

Kasworm, C. "Adult Student Identity in an Intergenerational Community College Classroom." *Adult Education Quarterly,* 2005, *56*(1), 3–20.

Kasworm, C. "Being Invisible and a Minority: Adult Undergraduates in a University." Paper presented at the American Education Research Association Conference, San Francisco, Apr. 2006.

Kasworm, C., Polson, C., and Fishback, S. *Responding to Adult Learners in Higher Education.* Malabar, Fla.: Krieger Publishing, 2002.

Mezirow, J., and Associates (eds.). *Learning as Transformation: Critical Perspectives on a Theory in Progress.* San Francisco: Jossey-Bass, 2000.

Pepin, Y. "Practical Knowledge and School Knowledge: A Constructivist Representation of Education." In M. Larochelle, N. Bednarz, and J. Garrison (eds.), *Constructivism and Education.* Cambridge: Cambridge University Press, 1988.

Taylor, K. "Autonomy and Self-Directed Learning: A Developmental Journey." In C. Hoare (ed.), *Handbook of Adult Development and Learning.* New York: Oxford University Press, 2006.

CAROL E. KASWORM is department head and professor in the Department of Adult and Higher Education at North Carolina State University.

New Directions for Adult and Continuing Education • DOI: 10.1002/ace

4

The rapid growth of online collaborative learning presents emotional challenges to students and adult educators. This chapter discusses two of these issues: epistemic and identity challenge.

Adult Learning and the Emotional Self in Virtual Online Contexts

Regina O. Smith

The online environment represents one of the fastest growing contexts for adult learning. Whereas online programs were uncommon ten years ago, almost all U.S. higher education institutions now offer them (Allen and Seaman, 2007). Enrollments in online courses continue to grow at rates far exceeding the total higher education student populations. According to Allen and Seaman (2007), almost 3.5 million students take at least one online course. Most of the growth comes from new higher education institutions that spring up to take advantage of the competition for adult students. Online courses and programs are also becoming increasingly popular ways to pursue professional development and deliver programs for academically underprepared adults.

The first online programs resembled electronic versions of old correspondence study programs (Boshier, Mohapi, and Boulton, 1997). As problems of low motivation, alienation, dissatisfaction, and attrition within these programs mounted, practitioners and scholars recommended more emphasis on building online learning communities through collaborative learning methods (Harasim, 1987). However, the emotional issues in collaborative learning associated with group process and development, communicating with peers to make decisions and solve problems, and developing relationships are largely ignored. The lack of attention to this issue may in fact sabotage the benefits of collaborative effort in online learning.

This chapter explores two issues that represent powerful emotional challenges for students in online collaborative learning groups: epistemic

NEW DIRECTIONS FOR ADULT AND CONTINUING EDUCATION, no. 120, Winter 2008 © 2008 Wiley Periodicals, Inc.
Published online in Wiley InterScience (www.interscience.wiley.com) • DOI: 10.1002/ace.314

and identity challenges. The chapter examines the theory of group and individual development, explores the emotional issues students face in online groups, looks at the ways in which these emotional issues facilitate adult and group development, and identifies some implications for adult educators.

The Group and the Individual

In the sense being used here, collaborative learning consists of small groups of students who work together on ill-structured problems to both co-construct knowledge and share classroom authority (Bruffee, 1999). The potential benefits to collaborative learning include increased learner motivation; the development of critical and problem-solving skills; and a social atmosphere where all learners can share, consider, challenge one another's ideas, and co-construct new knowledge (Bruffee, 1999). Attainment of these desired outcomes relies on a paradigmatic shift in learners' beliefs about teaching and learning. The old paradigm focuses on adult educators who transmit knowledge to learners. In the new paradigm, students learn through confronting and working through contextualized, ill-structured problems based on real-world practice, using resources appropriate to the subject being studied. The benefits of collaborative groups seem ideal for adult learning contexts, and research supports their usefulness (Bruffee, 1999).

This paradigmatic shift and the underlying paradoxical tensions inherent in all group work create considerable emotional tensions for the individual and between the individual and the group (Smith and Berg, 1987). Effective collaborative learning requires considerable interpersonal interaction to consider the other's point of view and work toward intersubjective agreement. These tasks rely on a well-developed and differentiated sense of self-other relations (Dirkx and Deems, 1994), fostered through individuation and group development.

As unique living entities, small groups grow and develop much like individuals (Wheelan, 1994). Just as development of the adult individual involves differentiation and separation from early childhood relationships, individuating and nurturing the development of a personal identity within the group represents the central issue for groups and individuals within the group (Bennis and Shepard, 1956; Smith and Berg, 1987). Group membership generates unconscious tension around conflicting fears of deindividualization (fusion with the group) or of alienation and estrangement from the group. Individuals crave the possibility for self-expression that they gain in association with one another. Yet when they require the company of others, humans submit to the threat of suppression, conformity, and constraint. Individuals fear that their lack of control may lead to dependence, which may submerge their individual identity under group identity and social roles. This tension is extremely emotionally laden and usually

New Directions for Adult and Continuing Education • DOI: 10.1002/ace

unconscious. Therefore, in such situations, individuals tend to either hold back or withdraw to eliminate the tension.

According to Smith and Berg (1987), while the individual member tries to avoid the tension, the group pressures the members to give in to the conflict so that the group can manage their fears and move on to productive work. Opportunities for individuation and group membership remain possible when members explore the underlying fears that cause the tension (Smith and Berg, 1987).

Emotional Issues in Online Groups

Collaborative online learning groups manifest emotional issues associated with these processes in several ways (Dirkx and Smith, 2004; Smith, 2005; Smith and Dirkx, 2007). Working in these contexts evokes considerable emotional tensions around the challenge to epistemological assumptions created by the lack of traditional instruction and the fear of losing one's individual voice within the group setting. Developing a collaborative learning environment challenges group members' existing understandings of the authority of knowledge and what it means to come to know. To effectively engage in collaboration, teachers must share their classroom authority with students, students must accept the new authority, and group members must work interdependently and accept responsibility for one another's learning.

When students realize that the teacher will not play the traditional role, their epistemic assumptions are called into question (Bruffee, 1999). For example, in one online graduate student group, India found it difficult to move away from the teacher as the expert (Smith, 2005). She said, "I'm very entrenched in traditional learning, and it's been a real journey for me to come into this program and discover about collaborative learning." When she tries to get the teacher to take on a more traditional role and he refuses to do so, she complains: "I could ask him a question, but he would respond with three more questions. He never really got my question answered. Like he never wanted to be the expert; he always would say, 'You know, I'm not the expert.' And, to me I think I can buy that to a certain extent, but of course he's the expert; you know this is his area of concentration." India's response demonstrates that the teacher's voluntary deauthorization provokes and challenges her existing beliefs regarding knowledge authority and also precipitates considerable intrapsychic stress.

The second challenge that students in online collaborative groups face is to their identity. That is, as group members, the students fear losing their voice and thus their individuality. Students participating in e-learning groups express an awareness of and responsibility to the group and its need for a sense of the commons (Smith and Dirkx, 2007). This awareness, however, also reflects a lurking fear of losing their sense of voice. For example, Chris explained, "It is necessary to find a common ground amongst the members in order to proceed for the good of the group, not the individual."

India captures the tension poignantly: "Can you be an individual in a collaborative setting? That is the tension!"

This need to proceed for the good of the group creates tension for individual participants who need the group for the benefits it provides. Yet they also sense that by relying on the group, they lose the ability to fully meet their own needs as learners. One has to give up something to become a group member, thus threatening a loss of individuality. Learners struggle to address both the needs of the group and their own individual needs, a complex process characterized by powerful emotions and feelings. As if to compensate for this fear of loss of individuality and voice, some group members may insist that all voices be literally represented and recognized in the group's final product. While an admirable effort, this strategy often produces awkward and choppy written products that lack a sense of group coherence and voice.

This tension between the individual and the group as a whole fosters a sense of ambivalence among members regarding the value of being part of the group and its contribution to their learning experiences. Individual contributions are often transformed to create a new whole in effective collaborative groups who work to co-construct knowledge (Bruffee, 1999). Many recognize the importance of the commons within the group; however, it is difficult for them to let go of their sense of individuality to allow something new and different to emerge from their commitment to the group. As a result, the "commons" often reflects various contributions that individuals bring to the group, resulting in something that metaphorically resembles a garden salad.

The nature of online communication exacerbates this struggle between the individual and the group and frustrates learners' ability to deal with conflict. Even when group members want to challenge one another's contributions, they are often not sure how to do so through text. For example, Paul remarked, "It became hard for me to trust some people's work. And in a classroom environment I would feel comfortable challenging them and saying, 'This seems like out of left field. Can you clarify what you really mean?' It's harder to get to that, I think, in an online situation." Reluctant to work through the difficult issues associated with forming and using meaningful relationships to get the work done, group members often devise strategies to minimize these conflicts. However, in the long run the strategies were not conducive to group development and high levels of productivity.

The challenges to both one's epistemic beliefs and one's identity are indicative of adult and group developmental issues.

Adult and Group Development in Online Small Groups

Many theorists, such as Bennis and Shepard (1956), suggest that as groups develop, they first face and work through issues of authority and then issues of intimacy. These issues reflect two distinct phases of group life: dependency on traditional authority and interdependency in which groups form an internal authority system. The simultaneous need to confront the developmental levels of epistemological development and the developmental needs of the group, however, exacerbate the emotional difficulties students face in online groups (Smith and Dirkx, 2007). That is, students in online collaborative groups need to deal with authority and intimacy at the same time.

Ideally, collaborative learning and the need to embrace the ambiguity of learning through ill-structured problems within the small groups should result in a paradigmatic shift from reliance on the teacher as knowledge creator to the small group as knowledge co-constructors. Participants, however, are overwhelmed with the need to authorize one another because of their differing self-authorship issues. Self-authorship is the ability to see oneself as an active knowledge creator and the ability to distinguish one's own thoughts and feelings from those of others within the learning context (Kegan, 1982, 1994). During early stages, learners view the teacher as the transmitter of knowledge and themselves as a passive recipient of the teacher's knowledge. The ability to evaluate differing view points is limited.

Epistemological development represents movement toward more complex knowledge views, a focus on the evaluation of different view points, and the ability to perceive oneself as a knowledge creator. Kegan (1982, 1994) suggests that the process of epistemological development reflects a cyclical nature of epistemological beliefs. Learners who participate in collaborative learning that requires them to learn the content among peers without traditional instruction may experience an imbalance between their beliefs and the demands of new learning expectations. This imbalance can create a strong emotional need that sometimes forces learners to retreat and reexamine their beliefs and assumptions about knowing and the nature of knowledge.

Yet the need to complete the work task remains. As students engage one another to address the group's tasks, they again confront the challenge to their beliefs. As they proceed with collaborative learning and seek to make decisions, they again find the challenge overwhelming and withdraw. This movement away from and toward the challenge represents developmental possibilities and movement toward acceptance of new epistemological assumptions needed to make the paradigmatic shift toward self-authorship. As India suggested, "It's been a real journey for me. . . . I am struggling and I am trying." At the same time that students face individual development opportunities, the group as a whole faces simultaneous opportunities for its own development.

As members of the group seek to connect and separate from the group, group development also resembles these pendulum swings. These dynamics and processes that are characteristic of the process of individuation in face-to-face groups (Gibbard, 1974) are also reflected in online groups

(Smith, 2005; Smith and Dirkx, 2007). Group processes tend to alternate between fears of fusion with the group and fears of alienation from the group. This continuing process contributes to subsequent differentiation of individual members from the group as a whole, as well as the establishment of effective interpersonal relationships between individual members and the group.

Fears of alienation and fusion are the two extreme ends of a continuum, representing feelings that group members hold regarding their relationship with other members of the group and the group as a whole. The alienation side of the continuum represents perceived relationships in which the individual group member is completely isolated and estranged from the group and his or her fellow group members. The fusion side represents perceived relationships in which the individual group members' identities merge completely with the group, and they lose a sense of who they are as an individual member. Group development reflects a pendulum that swings back and forth between these two extremes, with individuals gradually becoming more of who they are as group members and toward self-authorship.

The participants enter the group as individuals, but in the initial stages of the group, they seek to blend into the group so they will not stand out and risk rejection or estrangement. As the group continues to meet, however, the members perceive another risk: by avoiding the possibility of standing out in the group, they risk not being heard. That is, participants perceive the group as potentially suffocating them and obliterating their identity, and they experience a fear of fusion with the group (Gibbard, 1974). These conflicting emotions cause them to pull away from the group and seek independence. They want to preserve their individual uniqueness, but as they insist on the individual and unique aspects of their membership, the process evokes fears of alienation, of being disconnected and excluded from the group.

These dynamics are reflected in the descriptions of online group members' experience. For example, Paul explains, "I feel a little bit lost. . . . In my course work, I feel alone." Yet as Cynthia observes, moving toward connectedness with the members of the group creates additional frustration: "I don't like attachment. I really don't. I really like being by myself. I don't like having too many expectations placed on me from others in a social setting." Moving away from the group, however, generates new feelings of alienation and causes group members to move back toward the group. Participants seem to anticipate the benefits they derive from being a group member and again begin to feel safe in the context of the group.

Throughout their life cycle, online groups continue this back-and-forth movement between fusion and alienation, and the group as a whole gradually individuates (Boyd, 1991; Gibbard, 1974). That is, members of the group eventually engage in less fearful behavior and begin to act more out of an authentic sense of themselves as group members. Fears of alienation and fusion gradually decline, and as the group matures, these fears play less and less of a role over time. As this process occurs over time, groups generally become more effective and productive, a sign of a well-developed and mature group.

Implications for Adult and Continuing Education

The students in the online collaborative groups discussed in this chapter faced two simultaneous issues that are emotionally challenging and powerfully developmental. Practitioners in adult and continuing education play a key role in helping individuals and groups constructively address these issues.

To help facilitate group process and help the students address the epistemic and identity challenges, the instructor can implement several strategies. First, the instructor can create information for the course orientation. This information can include tips for being an effective group member, with emphasis on the need to fully discuss issues and not to withhold their opinions from the group. In this way, the groups can begin to address the fear of losing one's voice. Although this fear is largely unconscious, the teacher can help the group members recognize the need to voice this fear to the others. Usually group members find out that the other group members share this fear. Second, the instructor can help the group create ground rules for communication, with items such as how often members will check the discussion boards and respond to any messages, what to do if a member is unable to meet a group deadline or attend a group meeting, how to disagree with a group member's contribution without attacking the individual, and how to alert the group if the group member is unable to find the information the others requested. These ground rules create the perception that the group is able to move forward and hold one another accountable for their behavior. When disagreements arise, the groups can refer back to the ground rules for resolution. When the group is able to resolve an issue, the members are able to move closer to interdependence and are less fearful of losing their identity.

The instructor can help facilitate the paradigmatic move from total reliance on the teacher as knowledge creator to reliance on the group as knowledge co-creators by providing appropriate feedback during the process. Such feedback, for example, around discussion of the problem, the literature being used to help understand the problem, and the resolution, helps group members gain confidence about their interpretations of the problem and the literature. The feedback can include asking probing questions, encouraging the group members to share stories, and opportunities for reflection that link the course content to the students' lives.

Although these strategies help with conscious aspects of group work, they cannot adequately address the unconscious issues that also contribute to the two emotional challenges the online collaborative groups face. That is, rational strategies cannot always address the emotional issues the groups face. When the issues are largely unconscious but interfere with group work, the instructor will need to help the group identify the issue and then turn the problem back to the group for resolution.

In a recent online course, two of the three group members began attacking one another. One felt that the other was not contributing according to the group assignments, and the other member felt that the complaining member was being dominating. It turned out that the member who was not contributing had some fears about posting her ideas online. The other group members assured her that they felt her contributions were very valuable and that they really needed her to contribute. The fear of posting her ideas on the discussion board was so strong that she became emotionally overcome to tears when she thought about the problem. The group was able to move forward until they faced another conflict. This example illustrates that sometimes the problem is unconscious and the instructor may need to help the group identify the issue so that they can address it. Moreover, since groups often need to struggle and go through some difficult periods, teachers need to trust the group process to work. They can develop this trust by learning to appropriately analyze or diagnose the group's progress (Dirkx and Smith, 2004).

References

Allen, I. E., and Seaman, J. *Online Nation: Five Years of Growth in Online Learning.* Needham, Mass.: Sloan Consortium, 2007.

Bennis, W. G., and Shepard, A. H. "A Theory of Group Development." *Human Relations,* 1956, 9, 415–445.

Boshier, R., Mohapi, M., and Boulton, G. "Best and Worst Dressed Web Courses: Strutting into the 21st Century in Comfort and Style." *Distance Education,* 1997, 18(2), 327–349.

Boyd, R. D. *Personal Transformation in Small Groups: A Jungian Perspective.* London: Routledge, 1991.

Bruffee, K. A. *Collaborative Learning: Higher Education, Interdependence, and the Authority of Knowledge.* (2nd ed.) Baltimore, Md.: Johns Hopkins University Press, 1999.

Dirkx, J. M., and Deems, T. A. "The Influence of Self-Other Relationships in Constructivist Approaches to Adult Learning." Paper presented at the Midwest Research to Practice in Adult, Continuing, and Community Education, University of Wisconsin–Milwaukee, Oct. 1994.

Dirkx, J. M., and Smith, R. O. "Thinking Out of a Bowl of Spaghetti: Learning to Learn in Online Collaborative Groups." In T. Roberts (ed.), *Online Collaborative Learning: Theory and Practice.* Hershey, Pa.: Idea Group, 2004.

Gibbard, G. S. "Individuation, Fusion, and Role Specialization." In G. S. Gibbard, J. J. Hartman, and R. D. Mann (eds.), *Analysis of Groups.* San Francisco: Jossey-Bass, 1974.

Harasim, L. "Teaching and Learning On-Line: Issues in Computer-Mediated Graduate Courses." *Canadian Journal of Educational Communication,* 1987, 16(2), 117–135.

Kegan, R. (1982). *The Evolving Self: Problem and Process in Human Development.* Cambridge, Mass.: Harvard University Press, 1982.

Kegan, R. *In over Our Heads: The Mental Demands of Modern Life.* Cambridge, Mass.: Harvard University Press, 1994.

Smith, K. K., and Berg, D. N. *Paradoxes of Group Life: Understanding Conflict, Paralysis, and Movement in Group Dynamics*. Lanham, Md.: Lexington Books, 1987.

Smith, R. O. "Working with Difference in Online Collaborative Groups." *Adult Education Quarterly,* 2005, 55(3), 182–199.

Smith, R. O., and Dirkx, J. M. "Making the Invisible Visible: The Problem of Group Process in Online Collaborative Learning." Paper presented at the Organization for Promoting Understanding of Society Conference, London, England, Nov. 16–17, 2007.

Wheelan, S. A. *Group Processes: A Developmental Perspective*. Needham Heights, Mass.: Allyn and Bacon, 1994.

REGINA O. SMITH is an assistant professor of adult and continuing education within the Department of Administrative Leadership in the College of Education at the University of Wisconsin–Milwaukee.

New Directions for Adult and Continuing Education • DOI: 10.1002/ace

The authors use personal stories to discuss how race affects classroom dynamics and student interactions. In this chapter they focus on the role of emotions in the teaching-learning exchange, providing recommendations and strategies for fostering multiculturalism in the classroom.

Fostering Awareness of Diversity and Multiculturalism in Adult and Higher Education

Lisa M. Baumgartner, Juanita Johnson-Bailey

Multiculturalism and diversity are often discussed in tandem. Indeed it is difficult to discuss one without clarifying the meaning of the other. This conversation can be further complicated by the emotional reactions that often accompany the exchange. In this chapter, we offer practical and educational-centered working definitions of diversity and multiculturalism, and we also explore how emotions can influence dialogues, curriculum, and classroom experiences.

This chapter focuses on how race and ethnicity affect the educational process in the adult education classroom, including the role of emotions. We do not mean to imply that race and ethnicity are the only salient issues affecting our society. However, this chapter uses race as the lens through which to discuss how the positionality of students and teachers, their resulting understanding and beliefs, and the attached emotionality can affect the classroom. We include a brief discussion of how the intersection of other positionalities also affects the educational dynamic.

The term *diversity* generally refers to race, gender, age, and sexual orientation. Griggs (1995) classified diversity into primary and secondary dimensions. Primary dimensions are those human differences that are inborn that have an ongoing impact throughout our lives. There are six of them: age, ethnicity, gender, physical abilities and qualities, race, and sexual and affectional orientation. These primary dimensions cannot be changed, and they play a pivotal role in how we see ourselves and in how

others see and behave toward us. Multiculturalism flows from the examination of how diversity affects education: the classroom, curriculum, research, and literature. In addition, multiculturalism, as we perceive it, has at its core a political agenda and purpose: working within the educational system to foster an awareness and appreciation of diversity.

Race and ethnicity act in concert to determine how our society functions. Racial privilege and racial discrimination are manifested in customs, traditions, and norms. When a person is categorized as belonging to a race, that person is also accorded all the rights, privileges, and baggage that accompany the classification. Although race is socially constructed and is not the only positionality that categorizes or affects the social order, it is an important factor in the rankings that regulate societal hierarchy. The effects of how race and ethnicity are viewed in the world are embedded in our educational fabric, and the field of adult education is no exception.

The demographics on college campuses are increasingly diverse. More women are enrolling in college than men; enrollment of persons twenty-five years and older in college is expected to increase by 32 percent between 1990 and 2014; and the number of women in graduate school has exceeded men's enrollment since 1984 (National Center for Education Statistics, 2006). In 2004 minorities were 30 percent of American college students, up 15 percent since 1994. Although the rising numbers of Latino/as and Asians are responsible for much of the increase in diversity, the proportion of Black college students still rose from 9 percent in 1976 to 13 percent in 2004 (National Center for Education Statistics, 2006).

In short, we are dealing with a rapidly growing diverse society. Yet despite the inroads minorities have made on college campuses, the experiences of these students can still be one of isolation, alienation, and injury in the classroom (Marchesani and Adams, 1992). Although Whites often fail to recognize their White privilege, they still have the benefit of seeing their cultural norms universally valued, while people of color routinely sit in classrooms where they are missing from the curriculum and texts. However, people of color are routinely included in discussions by being singled out in the classroom to speak for "their" group. Moreover, students or faculty of color describe having their comments more often than not dismissed, interrupted, and not validated (Marchesani and Adams, 1992). This alienation for people of color occurs when the White, male, Western cultural norms of individuality, debate, and competitiveness, which are antithetical to the norms of many other cultures, dominate the classroom environment. For example, Asian students' values of "modesty, cooperation, and non-assertiveness" are adversative to the assertive or competitive culture of the American classroom (p. 12). Much of this traditional Western curriculum devalues the contributions and knowledge of others, further marginalizing minority students (Marchesani and Adams, 1992).

Due to their absence from the texts, implied worthlessness, and occasional stereotypical depiction, emotion-related injury can occur to those outside Lorde's (1995) mythical norm of White, male, heterosexual, Christian, and financially secure. For example, negative assumptions about intellect and competence are made about African Americans. Similarly, positive expectations are accorded to Asian students, who are often seen as being good at math and science. Moreover, a common mode of curriculum development that adds injury to insult is the exceptional outsider, which includes the contributions of those from marginalized groups according to traditionally accepted criteria. It is rare that marginalized voices are accepted as valid and more common for them to be measured against the standards of the dominant culture. Another format used in developing courses, a transformed curriculum, takes the ideas of the marginalized into account and encourages the questioning of assumptions, new ways of thinking, and new methodologies.

When there is so much emotion embedded in the teaching-learning transaction, how can we avoid the explosive pitfalls that occur in diversity classrooms in this Eurocentric institutional environment? How do we manage this in a world that privileges Western voices, knowledge, curriculum, and customs and disenfranchises Latino/as, African Americans, and Asians? First, we must recognize the spectrum of emotions that are part of every classroom experience: anxiety, excitement, fear, anger, apathy, shame, guilt, and joy. We know all too well from our own practices that anger and fear have derailed many diversity discussions. These two emotions can release hormones that affect learning and memory (Le Doux, 1996). People who feel attacked or unsafe may be unable to learn (Wolfe, 2006). In contrast, endorphins, which modulate emotions, help people feel good. Individuals remember learning experiences in environments that are welcoming, nurturing, and pleasant. If there is a sense of genuineness and empathy between the teacher and the learner, learning can flourish (Le Cornu and Collins, 2004). In addition, in a mildly stimulating environment, adrenaline is released, which increases learning (Wolfe, 2006).

The vignettes in the next section demonstrate how emotions enhance the teaching-learning transaction when dealing with issues of race, ethnicity, and White privilege and how emotionality may be used as a barrier to learning about racial discrimination in order to preserve White privilege.

Praxis in Action: A Review of the Practices of Two Adult Educators

We are a White adult educator (Lisa Baumgartner) and a Black adult educator (Juanita Johnson-Bailey), and we both teach core adult education courses or multicultural courses at predominantly White institutions in the Midwest and Southeast. Each of us teaches a diverse student population and offers examples here from our classes concerning or exploring how our positionality has affected our teaching and classroom interactions; how marginalized students often interact with the curriculum, teacher, and other students; and how students resist antiracist education.

Classroom Interactions and Race. So that our readers will better understand that we are all teachers and learners, each with our shoulders to the plow, we expose the underbellies of our practices. From our stories, we hope that you can see that we all struggle and improvise; sometimes we get it right, and sometimes we get it wrong. There are times when managing means just keeping our spirits up and laughing at the dilemmas that this dynamic topic engenders.

Lisa's Story.   My positionalities as a petite, single, child-free White woman in her early forties affect my classroom interactions with students. For the purposes of this chapter, I will concentrate on my race.

My Whiteness enhances my credibility in the classroom. I am rarely forced to consider how my race may affect students' perceptions of me. If I am challenged repeatedly in the classroom, I assume it is because I am young looking or female. I can make mistakes in the classroom and not be penalized or questioned. Furthermore, when I talk about racial discrimination and White privilege, I sometimes have students comment, "Why do you talk about that so much?" They rarely accuse me of having a personal agenda. Although some White students resist the data I present regarding how Blacks are treated by police and the health care and housing disparities between Blacks and Whites regardless of socioeconomic status, this resistance is due to their need to preserve White privilege.

Sometimes students appear angry at me for introducing topics that may be disorienting. Dirkx (2006) notes that emotions such as anger may be expressions of "unconscious psychic conflicts" (p. 16). Although the anger might be directed toward me as the instructor, students might just feel inadequate or may resist learning because of deeper emotional issues. So as an instructor, I sometimes attend to those emotions and work at deconstructing their origin, or I suggest that students journal about their thoughts. However, because of my White privilege, I know that I do not have to engage in as much emotional work and "emotional management strategies" (Harlow, 2003, p. 348) as my colleagues of color do. In addition, I can more easily channel the racist comments from students into questions because their comments are apart from who I am as a White person.

Once students work through their anger, guilt, and sadness, they sometimes want to learn more about a previously emotionally challenging topic. In this instance, positive emotions such as excitement and joy motivate them to pursue further learning on their own. I have had students wrestle with concepts in class and return to me a year or two later with a new understanding of racism or White privilege after their own self-directed reading and thinking on the topic.

Juanita's Story.   I am a Black woman adult educator whose life was kissed and enhanced by two of the greatest movements of the twentieth century: the civil rights and women's movements. As someone who has chosen to teach multiculturalism, my enthusiasm and political agenda shine through the curriculum. I see myself as a practitioner who uses humor and constructive confrontation to carry the class discussion across the difficult terrain of discussing the sensitive issues. My voice is more often soft than loud, my southern accent noticeable, and my dialogue peppered with colloquial sayings, mother wit, and frequent laughter. However, what has proven most disconcerting to me is that often this is not how I am seen by others. My positionalities, race, age, and gender, along with their accompanying stereotypes, influence how others see me.

Sometimes students assume that I am an affirmative action hire, that scholarship does not undergird my teaching, and that my personal connection and possible benefit from teaching about race drive my teaching. Anger, which is then manifested as resistance, often results from such assumptions. Other culprits are the latent emotions and suspicions connected to the American debate around affirmative action and the guilt and shame connected to the country's legacy regarding race and gender.

My first class of the semester always contains icebreakers around the subject of racism, sexism, or one of the so-called big five (as covered by Title VII): race, gender, sex, color, national origin, and religion. In one exercise, students are asked to raise their hands if they have ever done anything racist or sexist. My hand is the first to go up, followed by the confessed details of my latest faux pas. This technique lets students know that this classroom will not harbor shame, guilt, or blame, since we have been all socialized in an American society that infects us with the virus racism and sexism.

Yet notwithstanding my best intentions, some students are defensive and challenging. Here are standard comments that I receive:

"My family never owned slaves."
"We should not focus on the past. It just makes everyone feel bad."
"I'm from the North, and we don't do that."
"Everyone knows that minorities and women have all the rights."
"What about Tiger Woods and Oprah?"

While other students will be silent, squirm in their seats, and avoid eye contact, some students drop the class or appear engaged and satisfied until they express their disapproval on the evaluations.

Marginalized Student Interaction in the Classroom. Our classrooms always contain two categories of learners and teachers, the enfranchised and the disenfranchised, and their accompanying experiences and baggage (McIntosh, 1995). Too many times we focus on the experiences of the majority student population without realizing that the multicultural classroom can be an uncomfortable place for students of color.

Lisa's Story.   Students who are marginalized because of race or positionality may feel isolated, sad, or angry when the course curriculum does not reflect their views or circumstances. Such emotions may impede learning;

New Directions for Adult and Continuing Education • DOI: 10.1002/ace

depending on student-teacher interaction, however, these feelings may be ameliorated or intensified. Although the field in which I teach is dominated by women as both teachers and students, some female students see me as a role model and are forthcoming because I am female. In addition, student-to-student interaction may be affected by positionalities.

Juanita's Story.   One would assume that students of color would breathe a sigh of relief when they know that a professor of color is teaching a class about diversity or when they take a class on diversity. However, the opposite could be true. Perhaps students may feel more obliged and pressured to participate because of the need to share the burden of proof with their professor of color. Also, since marginalized learners are often invisible on their campuses and in their classrooms (Suarez-Balcazar and others, 2003), they are usually in the spotlight only when the topic concerns diversity. The glare of the lights and center stage can be uncomfortable and unwelcome since at such times, discussions of the "other" are too frequently about deficiencies and abnormal patterns.

Luckily, many women and students of color enter a diversity course wanting space and time to examine the tough issues. After all, in most cases, the diversity course is an elective, and these learners come because they are members of the choir. Then the task facing the professor becomes orchestrating and blending the voices and making a place for all opinions, the negative ones and the positive ones, so that no one voice is privileged over the other.

Resistance to Antiracist Education.   There are three common reactions in our classroom when we teach diversity: students sing along, deny, or resist. The most difficult of these approaches to handle are the many guises of resistance and denial.

Lisa's Story.   For students, exposure to diversity issues, questions of power, and White privilege can be an emotional, disorienting experience. When I discuss diversity, particularly White privilege, White students often use various techniques to deny or minimize its existence. Denial is a strategy used in order to perhaps keep negative feelings at bay. A common technique is to use the color-blind approach. In this view, Whiteness is not racially marked, and everyone is equal. This allows Whites to disassociate themselves from racial privilege since many are not racially conscious. The idea that people can be racist challenges their moral sense of self (Srivastava, 2005).

Once the wall of denial begins to disintegrate and people begin to have an inkling of understanding of White privilege, White students may experience anger, sadness, or guilt. Anger may be expressed by comments such as, "I am the one discriminated against because of affirmative action." It has been my experience that when Whites realize the enormous problem of racism and White privilege, they engage in a discourse of self-absorption and obsessively focus on their feelings of White guilt or upset without moving on and seeing how White privilege affects the larger world. I have also had White students who focus on, weigh, or compare their other positionalities to race. For example, one White gay man always talked about his oppression as a gay man. This discourse of self-absorption impedes learning and preserves White privilege (Hytten and Warren, 2003). These emotions and techniques are used to evade real discussion about race and White privilege.

When White students get past the emotions that paralyze them, they can begin to tap into emotions that fuel their learning. They are excited about learning more and doing more to eradicate racism. Some may be inclined to save other Whites from racism and have an action plan, while others may just want to read more about racism and White privilege and do nothing. It is important to attend to students' emotions at these stages so they can perhaps work toward continuing to recognize their place in race and racism in the American story.

Juanita's Story. Resisters come in all colors and genders, and perhaps more challenging is the fact that they have many ways of operationalizing their resistance. I am most often surprised by the resisters whom I have assumed were like-minded because of their positionalities as people of color. When a young Black woman once challenged me, I was left stumbling in silence. I had just constructively challenged a young White male, who had come to my Multicultural Perspectives on Women's Lives course, wearing a Confederate flag t-shirt, by deconstructing the reasons for the Civil War and writing the significant historical facts on the board in an effort to remove the emotionality:

- It was not about states' rights.
- It was not an economic issue.
- It was about owning slaves and betraying the founding American principles.

Immediately, this young Black woman raised her hand. I thought she was going to applaud my efforts. Instead, she uttered these fatal words: "That was then. This is now. Give it a rest." As most of the choir sat there in utter horror and silence, I could only laugh and say, "Let's discuss that further tomorrow." But before dismissing the class for the day, I offered extra credit if the students would bring in information for the debate so that they could move beyond being passive participants. The next class I introduced a time line that evidenced the connection between "then and now." After all, it is also my job to listen and to meet learners where they are. We were all the better for this unexpected challenge.

Recommendations and Strategies

Fostering diversity and multiculturalism in adult and higher education classroom means constructively managing the emotions that accompany this territory. Here we address how to encourage student awareness and empowerment.

New Directions for Adult and Continuing Education • DOI: 10.1002/ace

Traditionally, emotions have been vilified in the learning process. They were to be kept "under control," and "negative emotions" such as anger and sadness were excluded. While it is important not to become mired in emotion while discussing challenging issues, it is equally important not to avoid such discussions and to acknowledge emotion as an important component of the learning. Negative emotions can be a catalyst to delve deeper into the underlying assumptions. Positive emotions can enhance the learning process. Moreover, emotions are always to be acknowledged, not judged.

We contend that emotions that are on display are a sign that students care and are engaged. When a student expresses a strong emotion, it is a good time to take an intellectual breather, not a break or a recess, and say, "Do you mind if we explore that?" "I missed that side of it," or "How about we step back from this emotional terrain and deconstruct this premise."

Take advantage of the energy that learners bring to your classroom even when it means departing from the syllabus. These rare challenging teachable moments should be embraced as opportunities to knock down walls. As reflective practitioners (Brookfield, 1995), we should discuss these trying times by debriefing with colleagues and journaling.

Conclusion

In fostering diversity in adult and higher education, it is important to prepare students for the range of emotions they may experience with a statement on your syllabus. This could prevent students from getting stuck in their emotions and not engaging in the work they need to do. At times it may be appropriate as the instructor to intervene and keep the discourse constructive. We have found success by inviting disengaged students to become self-directed and contribute readings, admitting that we do not have answers, and asking students to think aloud about possible solutions.

Knowing the volatility of teaching diversity courses, our design will always contain a variety of readings by Whites, people of color, men and women, multimedia, guest speakers, debriefing, group work free of teacher involvement, and a syllabus statement about risk. And finally, it is essential to be open and to let students know that you do not have—but are attempting to provide—a space where we all can learn and improve.

References

Brookfield, S. *Becoming a Critically Reflective Teacher*. San Francisco: Jossey-Bass, 1995.

Dirkx, J. "Engaging Emotions in Adult Learning: A Jungian Perspective on Emotion and Transformative Learning." In E. W. Taylor (ed.), *Teaching for Change: Fostering Transformative Learning in the Classroom*. New Directions for Adult and Continuing Education, no. 109. San Francisco: Jossey-Bass, 2006.

Griggs, L. B. "Valuing Diversity: Where from . . . Where to?" In L. B. Griggs and L. L. Louw (eds.), *Valuing Diversity: New Tools for a New Reality*. New York: McGraw-Hill, 1995.

Harlow, R. "'Race Doesn't Matter But . . .' The Effect of Race on Professors' Experiences and Emotion Management in the Undergraduate College Classroom." *Social Psychology Quarterly*, 2003, *66*(4), 348–363.

Hytten, K., and Warren, J. "Engaging Whiteness: How Racial Power Gets Reified in Education." *Qualitative Studies in Education*, 2003, *16*(1), 65–89.

Le Cornu, R., and Collins, J. "Re-Emphasizing the Role of Affect in Learning and Teaching." *Pastoral Care in Education*, 2004, *4*, 27–33.

Le Doux, J. *The Emotional Brain.* New York: Simon and Schuster, 1996.

Lorde, A. "Age, Race, Class, and Sex: Women Redefining Difference. In B. Guy-Sheftall (Ed.), *Words of Fire: An Anthology of African American Feminist Thought.* New York: New Press, 1995.

Marchesani, L. S., and Adams, M. "Dynamics of Diversity in the Teaching-Learning Process: A Faculty Development Model." In M. Adams (ed.), *Promoting Diversity in College Classrooms: Innovative Responses for the Curriculum, Faculty, and Institutions.* New Directions for Teaching and Learning, No. 52. San Francisco: Jossey-Bass, 1992.

McIntosh, P. "White Privilege and Male Privilege: A Personal Accounting of Coming to See Correspondences Through Work in Women's Studies." In M. L. Andersen and P. H. Collins (eds.), *Race, Class, and Gender: An Anthology.* (2nd ed.) Belmont, Calif.: Wadsworth, 1995.

National Center for Education Statistics. (2006). *Digest of Education Statistics, 2005.* Washington, D.C.: U.S. Department of Education. Retrieved Feb. 4, 2007, from http://nces.ed.gov/fastfacts/display.asp?id=98.

Srivastava, S. "'You're Calling Me a Racist?' The Moral and Emotional Regulation of Antiracism and Feminism." *Signs: Journal of Women in Culture and Society,* 2005, *31*(1), 29–62.

Suarez-Balcazar, Y., and others "Experiences of Differential Treatment Among College Students of Color." *Journal of Higher Education,* 2003, *71*(4), 428–444.

Wolfe, P. "The Role of Meaning and Emotion in Learning." In E. W. Taylor (ed.), *Teaching for Change: Fostering Transformative Learning in the Classroom.* New Directions for Adult and Continuing Education, no. 109. San Francisco: Jossey-Bass, 2006.

LISA M. BAUMGARTNER *is an associate professor in the adult and higher education program at Northern Illinois University.*

JUANITA JOHNSON-BAILEY *is a professor of adult education and women's studies at the University of Georgia.*

New Directions for Adult and Continuing Education • DOI: 10.1002/ace

6

The chapter examines learning and emotion at work and how emotional intelligence and emotion work affect well-being, identity development, and power relations. The chapter also considers how human resource development and emotion interact in learning, training, and change initiatives.

Adult Learning in the Workplace: Emotion Work or Emotion Learning?

Laura L. Bierema

Most of us have heard the advice, "Don't get too emotional," at some point during our work lives. Expressing emotion at work has historically been taboo. Although we may have perfected the poker face, our bodies and minds refuse to banish emotion from our repertoire. Organizational life evokes joy, hate, anger, despair, curiosity, and esteem, yet as far as management is concerned, emotions are disruptive, dysfunctional, and derailing.

In spite of managerial reluctance to embrace the emotional self as a relevant aspect of the worker, emotion makes us human, and organizations weigh on workers' emotional health. Work life is emotion laden, and emotional expression has become more accepted in U.S. organizations with the popularity of emotional intelligence as a core interpersonal competency. The concept was originated by Salovey and Mayer (1990) and popularized by Daniel Goleman in his book *Emotional Intelligence* (1995). The premise of emotional intelligence is that IQ comprises only a small portion of intelligence and that the ability to identify and manage one's emotions, and anticipate those of others, is a key interpersonal competency.

The surging popularity of emotion is based on its promise to improve worker productivity and retention, not necessarily because it will enhance well-being. Although the motives vary, emotion formation, expression, and control in the workplace is receiving increased attention (Callahan, 2002; Fineman, 2000; Sturdy, 2003; Tracy, 2000, 2005). Emotional intelligence results in lower absenteeism, better psychological health, higher commitment, clearer role boundaries, higher levels of responsibility and performance

NEW DIRECTIONS FOR ADULT AND CONTINUING EDUCATION, no. 120, Winter 2008 © 2008 Wiley Periodicals, Inc.
Published online in Wiley InterScience (www.interscience.wiley.com) • DOI: 10.1002/ace.316

of direct reports, higher satisfaction, and better coping skills (Sardo, 2004). It has also been advocated as enhancing organization learning (Singh, 2007), differentiating average from outstanding salespeople (Deeter-Schmelz and Sojka, 2003), and promoting higher levels of learning and teamwork (Sardo, 2004). In addition, it has been suggested that emotional intelligence can be developed, and that training is particularly effective at developing enabling aspects of emotional intelligence such as self-awareness, interpersonal sensitivity, and influence (Dulewicz and Higgs, 2004).

Although many organizations are jumping on the emotion bandwagon, workplace educators have a responsibility to examine emotional education and learning critically. Emotions are often regarded by management as something to be managed, manipulated, and controlled and as forces creating unwanted resistance to change as well as promoting productivity. Hochschild (1983) argued that emotion work—the expression of emotions as a condition of work that are not necessarily genuine, or may even be contrary to the true emotions of the employee—is a form of human exploitation that can cause feelings of alienation and ill health. Emotional work life is yet another site for the definition and reinforcement of power relations (Fineman, 2000). Emotion is at risk of becoming a commodity similar to the learning organization model that expects access to workers' thoughts, experiences, and emotions (Mojab and Gorman, 2003). Tending to emotional health and the work of employees for the motives of productivity may overlook workers' interests in favor of the organization. This chapter examines learning and emotion at work; considers well-being, identity development, and power relations; and explores how workplace educators can respond through training and change initiatives.

Emotion and Learning in the Workplace

Emotional learning involves meddling with deeply personal, private aspects of workers' lives in an effort to influence and shape their emotions, sometimes with constructive and sometimes with destructive results. Two aspects of emotion have particular relevance in the workplace: emotional intelligence and emotion labor.

Salovey and Mayer (1990) define emotional intelligence as the ability to monitor one's own emotions, discriminate between positive and negative emotions, and use emotional knowledge to guide thought and action. They suggest that emotional intelligence incorporates perception, assimilation, understanding, and management of emotions.

The concept of emotion work or emotion labor (Hochschild, 1983) views emotion as a core dimension of work and a new factor of production requiring emotion regulation and expression. Emotion labor is an "organizationally prescribed display of feeling" (Tracy, 2005, p. 261). Jobs requiring emotion labor have three key characteristics:

New Directions for Adult and Continuing Education • DOI: 10.1002/ace

First, they require face-to-face or voice-to-voice contact with the public. Second, they require the worker to produce an emotional state in another person—gratitude or fear for example. Third, they allow the employer, through training and supervision, to exercise a degree of control over the emotional activities of employees [Hochschild, 1983, p. 17].

Emotion labor requires workers to emote states that may be inconsistent with their authentic feelings. Service workers, for example, are required to project a pleasant demeanor (Tracy, 2000), and other workers, such as firefighters (Scott and Myers, 2005) and 911 dispatchers (Tracy and Tracy, 1998), must remain calm during emergencies. Emotion work has been extended from customer interactions to coworker interactions (Tschan, Rochat, and Zapf, 2005), with emotion factoring into job evaluations, organizational change, and interpersonal relationships.

Emotion labor is characterized by additional features of display rules, authenticity, emotional dissonance, and deviance. Display rules are implicit or explicit norms of behavior often conveyed through training and socialization. For instance, Disney's expectations are "first we practice the friendly smile at all times with our guests and among ourselves" (Rafaeli and Sutton, 1987, as cited in Tschan, Rochat, and Zapf, 2005, p. 195). Emotion work requires emoting with authenticity. Yet the visibly happy employee may be feeling detachment or annoyance, essentially faking emotions to comply with work requirements. This discrepancy between felt and displayed emotion is called emotional dissonance, or the frequency of having to display emotions that oppose true feelings, such as being pleasant to a rude customer.

Lewig and Dollard (2003) confirmed that emotional dissonance was the key factor contributing to job exhaustion and job satisfaction. Emotional dissonance has been linked with ill health (Morris and Feldman, 1996; Zapf, 2002) and a loss of the capacity to regulate one's emotions (Dollard and others, 2003), and hiding negative emotions results in burnout (Brotheridge and Grandey, 2002). Imbalance between dissonance and rewards (esteem, money, security) creates even more emotional exhaustion and dissatisfaction among call center workers than just the emotional dissonance by itself (Lewig and Dollard, 2003). Deviance occurs when workers deviate from display rules and emote an authentically felt emotion, such as rolling one's eyes in front of the customer or saying something inappropriate rather than the required emotion. Dissonance tends to characterize interactions with customers, while deviance more likely characterizes coworker interactions (Tschan, Rochat, and Zapf, 2005).

Well-Being. Although emotion has become trendy in organizations, its role in the overall well-being of workers is generally overlooked. Workplaces are sites of stress, toxicity, burnout, and uncertainty. Work evokes a range of emotions and experiences for workers where customers demand dependability, promptness, value, pleasing physical amenities (facilities, materials), and individual attention (Parasuraman, Zeithaml, and Barry, 1988). Colleagues demand collegiality and teamwork, and the environment can be oppressive in ways that marginalize and diminish workers' sense of self and well-being. Organizations can also provide emotional highs, including high levels of personal accomplishment, advancement, collaboration, and recognition.

Foss (2007) defines well-being as the absence of work-related stress, being happy and satisfied at work, working to full potential, and feeling empowered. She charges productivity-centered approaches to innovation and change as becoming the discourse of organizational health: "Employees' hearts, minds, and now health and well-being are raw capital to be harnessed and subjugated to organizational interests" (p. 12).

Burnout is another factor that erodes emotional well-being and is a feature of emotion work. It is the inability to manage emotions in interactions with customers and a syndrome of emotional exhaustion, depersonalization, and low personal accomplishment (Maslach, 1982; Zapf and others, 2001). Job stressors include role conflict, role stress, stressful events, workload, depersonalization, and work pressure (Zapf and others, 2001). Emotion work contributes to job dissatisfaction, absenteeism, turnover, and burnout (Zapf and others, 2001).

Identity Development. Emotion work affects identity. Demanding work life can dictate emotions to the point that the employee becomes confused about his or her real feelings since they must be carefully controlled on the job (Bergquist, 1993). Training to do these jobs (such as flight attendant and bill collector) is comparable to the deep acting taught to actors:

> Unfortunately, when these employees become skillful at such management, they can no longer rely on their emotions to provide them with an accurate sense of their real attitudes, values, and feelings about other people or events. They have learned how to con themselves, and no longer know who they really are [pp. 72–73].

Ashforth and Humphey (1993) suggest that emotional labor allows workers to become efficient with tasks and self-expression, but simultaneously creates unrealistic customer expectations that may trigger emotional dissonance and self-alienation. Drawing on social identity theory, they argue that some effects of emotional labor are moderated by one's social and personal identities and that emotional labor stimulates pressures for the person to identify with the service role. Identification with false roles causes stress and burnout and has a negative impact on well-being.

Ackerman and Maslin-Ostrowski (2004) interviewed sixty-five school leaders across the United States and concluded that wounding experiences (vulnerability, isolation, fear, and power) provide opportunities to question one's leadership and provide important social and emotional learning,

New Directions for Adult and Continuing Education • DOI: 10.1002/ace

affirming the importance of emotion to leadership, particularly during times of crisis. Callahan and McCollum (2002) note that during change initiatives, many organizations create unrealistic expectations for employee support and loyalty, yet what is needed are opportunities for dialogue and a sense that individual identity will be preserved in the midst of change. Emotion labor that creates cognitive dissonance erodes workers' internal resources. Dormann and Zapf (2004) note that customer interactions that threaten a worker's self-esteem and hinder the development of good relations or those that create feelings of insecurity are particularly damaging.

Emotion and Power Relations. Learning about emotion is shaped by the particular context and is an important element of socialization into all types of social membership (Rustin, 2003). "The formal (and informal) techniques of control—such as appraisal procedures, surveillance methods, performance assessments, rules of negotiation—are organizational phenomena that are lived through feelings of being controlled or controlling others" (Fineman, 2000, pp. 7–8). Fineman observes how emotions of fear, anxiety, or disdain can be exploited in organizations. Power is malleable, linked to feelings of fear, humiliation, pride, and achievement. Like power, emotions are fluid, continually in a state of flux and negotiation. They are shaped by the past and present, with history creating memories in individuals, groups, and organizations that influence their interactions. Emotions are also a means of reproducing social structures of sexism, racism, and classism in organizations. Emotions have been used as a means of appearing more powerful, masculine, and rational (Buzzanell and Turner, 2003; Mumby and Putnam, 1992), and emotional learning at work may signal unconscious issues that all workers deal with, such as identity, power, conflict, teamwork, and marginalization. Emotion can be manipulated to preserve power relations, and women tend to be segregated in jobs that require higher degrees of emotion work, particularly in the service industry. Service workers are often instructed that the customer is always right and are forced to accommodate rudeness, harassment, and sometimes sexual advances (Price, 2008), while also accepting lower pay and fewer options for advancement. Opengart (2003) interviewed women managers and concluded that expectations for emotional expression are gendered, and the nature of patriarchy may require women to engage in more emotion work since women are expected to emulate masculine traits, and the social structure is replicated through emotional expression. She concluded that emotional intelligence and emotion work frame emotional learning in the workplace and influence worker well-being, identity development, socialization, and power relations.

Human Resource Development and Emotion

This chapter has shown how organizations seek to harness emotion and emotion work to advance organization goals. Although promoting emotional well-being has potential benefit, profit motives threaten to commodify and manipulate the emotional lives of workers. Emotional health is a component of organization well-being, which consists of healthy, satisfied workers who are fully employed in an organization that is meeting stakeholder needs. Human resource development (HRD) is in a position to consider emotional learning beyond specific jobs or performance goals in the context of promoting organization well-being.

The delicacy of emotion learning must be considered first at the organization level, where management needs to grapple with the consequences of emotion work and attempt to provide workers with coping strategies and resources to address emotional stress. Goldman Schuyler (2004) suggests leaders must attend to vision, teamwork, and individual development when promoting organization well-being. Organizations must provide more resources for workers in intense emotion work roles, including support and control. Dollard and others (2003) suggest that although service jobs can be stressful, access to resources such as security, a sense of relatedness, self-esteem, autonomy, mastery, and personal growth can buffer customer demands. The real or anticipated absence of such resources causes psychological strain.

The work of both management and HRD is emotion laden, and Goldman Schuyler (2004) notes that workers who serve as buffers between management and workers are

> attempting to catalyze change needs to sustain their own wellbeing at deep levels. . . . Unless organizational development consultants increase their ability to manage their deeper levels of health, they risk becoming "toxic handlers" who assist an organization in being healthy by channeling toxicity, rather than by helping it to transform itself in significant ways [pp. 28–29].

A "toxic handler" is "a manager who voluntarily shoulders the sadness, frustration, bitterness, and anger that are endemic to organizational life" (Frost and Robinson, 1999, p. 98). Frost and Robinson view the presence of toxic handlers as a necessary evil in organizations characterized by high levels of creative and strategic work. Goldman Schuyler notes that the work of toxic handling results in burnout, stress, and physical illness. Her own poignant account of becoming ill after engaging in toxic handling is a testament to the documented effects of its damage to the immune system. Drawing on Frost and Schein, Goldman Schuyler observes, "One must learn how to spend considerable time immersed in unhealthy environments without being influenced by them in negative ways" (p. 30). Such skills require high levels of emotional intelligence and work. Training and organization change initiatives affect workers and the toxic handlers assigned to facilitate and manage such work.

Training and Emotional Learning. Workplace educators play a significant role in emotion learning, and formal training may be provided to improve emotional intelligence or teach appropriate emotional responses. Rustin (2003) suggests clarifying the emotional requirements of different tasks and functions and what educational strategies work best to address them. Training to cope with emotional dissonance has been effective in studies on flight attendants (Dormann and Kaiser, 2002), and appropriate customer-focused training might serve as an important resource to counter the negative impact of stressful emotion work. Other research has also shown that training serves as a "facilitative condition" in reducing job stress, along with appropriate leadership, information sharing, and feedback (Schneider & Bowen, 1993; Schneider, White, and Paul, 1998).

Short and Yorks (2002) examined the emotionality of training and submit that training context and participants govern appropriate emotional responses. They view trainers as theater performers who follow scripts (display rules) dictating their reaction to trainees and public management of their emotions, which often includes suppression. They recognize ways in which emotion inhibits learning for participants, including lack of confidence, fear of failure, fear of others' responses, grief over change, previous negative experiences, and the learner's emotional state. They advocate "whole person knowing" to facilitate emotions in the training process by establishing a climate of learning-within-relationship or engaging with the whole person based on empathy and mutuality. They recommend creating the right environment for discussing emotions and establishing a safe context for dialogue. They challenge trainers to explore their own emotions in developing understanding about the training topic and to self-disclose emotions and cater to individuals' different emotional needs.

Organization Change. Organizations tend to be places of uncertainty and change. Goldman Schuyler (2004) advocates that organizational practitioners are most effective when their change process includes skills in organizational change and business, a model for organizational health, and practical, theoretical approaches for maintaining individual health (encompassing physical, spiritual, and mental well-being).

Emotion is connected to change in organizations as organization life evokes emotion and relies on emotion work to get the job done. Kiefer (2002) notes that organizational literature focuses on rational and cognitive aspects of change, viewing emotions as expressions of human frailty requiring intervention. She contends that such a narrow view is superficial, limiting our understanding of emotion. Turnbull (2002) concludes that deliberate managing of emotion may result in unintended and unexpected emotions among participants in planned corporate change programs that make achieving intended outcomes more difficult.

Management often frames emotions as stress or resistance in the face of organization change and views common reactions of anger, distrust, and fear as irrational (Kiefer, 2002). What is often overlooked, however, is how emotion can be a catalyst for change. Organizations need to better understand this side of emotionality and tend to it when addressing change and uncertainty. Emotion must be valued as a valid and important aspect of change initiatives, not a force to be controlled and diminished. Kiefer (2002) recommends that management explore emotion and its role in meaning construction during change and consider it as an integral part of individual adaptation and motivation that is a social phenomenon. In fact, change is both an individual and a social phenomenon, and emotions are not destructive but a vital part of change. Emotions structure how people create meaning in the face of change and help people navigate change.

The emotional well-being of workers is a complex process that intersects with the organization culture, history, structure, policies, and politics. Emotion has a significant impact on well-being, identity development, and power relations. It is important to value and develop the emotional well-being of workers, but it should be done in conjunction with a broader commitment to promoting organizational well-being. As a strategy for addressing emotion, striving for overall organization well-being is preferred to piecemeal efforts to monitor, control, and shape the emotions of workers. Organization well-being holds the potential to have a positive impact on all facets of the organization and should be a driving goal when attempting to address emotional learning.

References

Ackerman, R. H., and Maslin-Ostrowski, P. "The Wounded Leader and Emotional Learning in the Schoolhouse." *School Leadership and Management*, 2004, *24*(3), 311–328.

Ashforth, B. E., and Humphrey, R. H. "Emotional Labor in Service Roles: The Influence of Identity." *Academy of Management Review*, 1993, *18*, 88–115.

Bergquist, W. *The Postmodern Organization: Mastering the Art of Invisible Change.* San Francisco: Jossey-Bass, 1993.

Brotheridge, C. M., and Grandey, A. A. "Emotional Labor and Burnout: Comparing Two Perspectives of 'People Work.'" *Journal of Emotional Behavior*, 2002, *60*, 17–39.

Buzzanell, P. M., and Turner, L. H. "Emotional Work Revealed by Job Loss Discourse: Backgrounding-Foregrounding of Feelings, Construction of Normalcy, and (Re)instituting of Traditional Masculinities." *Journal of Applied Communication Research*, 2003, *31*(1), 27–57.

Callahan, J. L. (ed.). "Perspectives of Emotion and Organizational Change." *Advances in Developing Human Resources*, 2002, *4*(1).

Callahan, J. L., and McCollum, E. E. "Conceptualizations of Emotion Research in Organizational Contexts." *Advances in Developing Human Resources*, 2002, *4*(1), 4–21.

Deeter-Schmelz, D. R., and Sojka, J. Z. "Developing Effective Salespeople: Exploring the Link Between Emotional Intelligence and Sales Performance." *International Journal of Organizational Analysis*, 2002, *11*(3), 211–220.

Dollard, M. F., and others. "Unique Aspects of Stress in Human Service Work." *Australian Psychologist*, 2003, *38*(2), 84–91.

Dormann, C., and Kaiser, D. "Job Conditions and Customer Satisfaction." *European Journal of Work and Organizational Psychology*, 2002, *11*, 257–283.

Dormann, C., and Zapf, D. "Customer Related Social Stressors and Burnout." *Journal of Occupational Health Psychology*, 2004, *9*(1), 61–82.

Dulewicz, V., and Higgs, M. "Can Emotional Intelligence Be Developed?" *International Journal of Human Resource Management*, 2004, *15*(1), 95–111.

Fineman, S. "Emotional Arenas Revisited." In S. Fineman (ed.), *Emotion in Organizations.* (2nd ed.) Thousand Oaks, Calif.: Sage, 2000.

Foss, K. M. "The Lived Experience of Well-Being and Learning in Organizations: The Story of Women." Unpublished doctoral dissertation, University of Alberta, 2007.

Frost, P., and Robinson, S. "The Toxic Handler." *Harvard Business Review,* 1999, 77(4), 96–107.

Goldman Schuyler, K. "Practitioner—Heal Thyself! Challenges in Enabling Organizational Health." *Organization Management Journal—Emerging Scholarship,* 2004, 1(1), 28–37.

Goleman, D. *Emotional Intelligence: Why It Can Matter More Than IQ.* New York: Bantam Books, 1995.

Hochschild, A. R. *The Managed Heart: The Commercialization of Human Feeling.* Berkeley: University of California Press, 1983.

Kiefer, T. "Understanding the Emotional Experience of Organizational Change: Evidence from a Merger." *Developing Human Resources,* 2002, 4(1), 39–61.

Lewig, K., and Dollard, M. F. "Can I Help You? Emotional Labor, Wellbeing, and Job Satisfaction Among Call Centre Workers." *European Journal of Work and Organizational Psychology,* 2003, 12, 366–392.

Maslach, C. *Burnout: The Costs of Caring.* Upper Saddle River, N.J.: Prentice Hall, 1982.

Mojab, S., and Gorman, R. "Women and Consciousness in the 'Learning Organization': Emancipation or Exploitation?" *Adult Education Quarterly,* 2003, 3(4), 228–241.

Morris, J. A., and Feldman, D. C. "The Dimensions, Antecedents, and Consequences of Emotional Labour." *Academy of Management Journal,* 1996, 21, 989–1010.

Mumby, D., and Putnam, L. "The Politics of Emotion: A Feminist Reading of Bounded Rationality." *Academy of Management Review,* 1992, 17(3), 465–486.

Opengart, R. A. "Women Managers: Learning About Emotional Expression in the Workplace." Unpublished doctoral dissertation, University of Georgia, 2003.

Parasuraman, A., Zeithaml, V. A., and Barry, L. L. "SERVQUAL: A Multiple-Item Scale for Measuring Consumer Perceptions of Service Quality." *Journal of Retailing,* 1988, 64, 12–40.

Price, T. A. "Women of the Hotel Front Office: Negotiating Difficult Guests." Unpublished doctoral dissertation, University of Georgia, 2008.

Rafaeli, A., and Sutton, R. I. "Expression of Emotion as a Part of the Work Role." *Academy of Management Review,* 1987, 12, 13–37.

Rustin, M. "Guest Editorial: Emotional Labour and Learning About Emotions." *European Journal of Psychotherapy, Counseling, and Health,* 2003, 6(3), 167–174.

Salovey, P., and Mayer, J. "Emotional Intelligence." *Imagination, Cognition and Personality,* 1990, 9, 185–211.

Sardo, S. "Learning to Display Emotional Intelligence." *Business Strategy Review,* 2004, 15(1), 14–17.

Schneider, B., and Bowen, A. E. "The Service Organization: Human Resources Management Is Crucial." *Organizational Dynamics,* 1993, 21, 39–52.

Schneider, B., White, S. S., and Paul, M. C. "Linking Service Climate and Customer Perceptions of Service Quality: Test of Causal Model." *Journal of Applied Psychology,* 1998, 83, 150–163.

Scott, C., and Myers, K. K. "The Socialization of Emotion: Learning Emotion Management at the Fire Station." *Journal of Applied Communication Research,* 2005, 33, 67–92.

Short, D. C., and Yorks, L. "Analyzing Training from an Emotions Perspective." *Advances in Developing Human Resources,* 2002, 4(1), 80–96.

Singh, S. K. "Role of Emotional Intelligence in Organisational Learning: An Empirical Study." *Singapore Management Review,* 2007, 29(2), 55–74.

Sturdy, A. "Knowing the Unknowable? A Discussion of Methodological and Theoretical Issues in Emotion Research and Organization Studies." *Organization,* 2003, 10, 81–105.

Tracy, S. J. "Becoming a Character for Commerce: Emotion Labor, Self-Subordination, and Discursive Construction of Identity in a Total Institution." *Management Communication Quarterly,* 2000, *14,* 90–128.

Tracy, S. J. "Locking Up Emotion: Moving Beyond Dissonance for Understanding Emotion Labor Discomfort." *Communication Monographs,* 2005, *72*(3), 261–283.

Tracy, S. J., and Tracy, K. "Emotion Labor at 911: A Case Study and Theoretical Critique." *Journal of Applied Communication Research,* 1998, *26,* 390–411.

Tschan, F., Rochat, S., and Zapf, D. "It's Not Only Clients: Studying Emotion Work with Clients and Co-Workers with an Event-Sampling Approach." *Journal of Occupational and Organizational Psychology,* 2005, *78,* 195–220.

Turnbull, S. "The Planned and Unintended Emotions Generated by a Corporate Change Program." *Advances in Developing Human Resources,* 2002, *4*(1), 22–38.

Zapf, D. "Emotion Work and Psychological Strain: A Review of the Literature and Some Conceptual Considerations." *Human Resource Management Review,* 2002, *12,* 237–268.

Zapf, D., and others. "Emotion Work and Job Stressors and Their Effects on Burnout." *Psychology and Health,* 2001, *16,* 527–545.

LAURA L. BIEREMA is associate professor of adult education and human resource and organization development at the University of Georgia.

New Directions for Adult and Continuing Education • DOI: 10.1002/ace

7

The arts engage our senses, provoking strong, affective responses for both the creator and the witness of art. Our emotions can provide a catalyst for informal adult learning beyond traditional, cognitive ways of knowing.

Powerful Feelings: Exploring the Affective Domain of Informal and Arts-Based Learning

Randee Lipson Lawrence

I am watching a performance of *"Cry" (For All Black Women Everywhere Especially Our Mothers)* by the Alvin Ailey American Dance Theater. Soloist Judith Jamison is tall and regal in a flowing white dress. With only her body as the tools of her art, synchronized with Alice Coltrane's sensuous jazz rhythms, she exquisitely takes us on a journey through the hardships of slavery and women's stories of pain, loss, sorrow, joy, and triumph of survival. I am riveted. I stop breathing. I feel a chill, and there is the heaviness of tears behind my eyes. I am not Black, my ancestors were not slaves, and at this time I have not yet given birth to a child. I am nonetheless deeply affected.

This chapter looks at the ways in which we learn informally through artistic expression such as dance, drama, poetry, music, literature, film, and all of the visual arts and how we access this learning through our emotions. We begin with a look at the limitations of relying primarily on technical-rational learning processes. Learning through the arts is then explored through the theoretical lenses of transformative, experiential, and indigenous learning. We next examine the affective domain of arts-based learning in teaching for social justice. Finally, implications for adult education are discussed.

The Case for Arts-Based Affective Knowing

Our dominant Western culture prizes rational-cognitive ways of knowing. In a milieu where logic rules and reason prevails, emotional and embodied

New Directions for Adult and Continuing Education, no. 120, Winter 2008 © 2008 Wiley Periodicals, Inc.
Published online in Wiley InterScience (www.interscience.wiley.com) • DOI: 10.1002/ace.317

ways of knowing are often dismissed and ignored. And yet we are all emotional beings. To suppress our emotions is not only unnatural; it prevents us from expressing our full humanness. Fortunately, educators like Dirkx (2001) and others are emphasizing the role of emotionality as an essential component of adult learning.

Hart (2000) discusses inspiration as an extrarational way of knowing that comes when we make this epistemic shift away from pure rational thinking. Inspiration, for Hart, is an emotional-cognitive process, or what he calls "full bodied knowing" (p. 39). He believes that our intellectual and emotional selves are deeply interconnected. "Inspiration is the poet in the process of learning, the prophet beholding the voice of God, the artist hearing the Muse, and the 'ordinary' person becoming, if only for a moment, extraordinary" (p. 33).

Art making is a deeply emotional and, some would say, spiritual process (Allen, 2005; Malchiodi, 2002; Wuthnow, 2001). Yet even art is often dominated by our rational mind. We carefully plan our projects, making sure to have the correct materials, the right timing, and the technical knowledge. Due to this pressure to produce great art, many of us who do not consider ourselves artists, poets, or actors refrain from engaging in these activities at all. But what if we embraced creative projects for their learning potential? What if we gave up on the need to be technically correct or to produce anything of value? What if we lived in the moment?

Letting go of technical rationality frees us to make space for sensory imagery in a world dominated by cognitive processes. In this space where senses are heightened and emotions run high, we sometimes go into an altered state, or flow. Csikszentmihalyi (1996) describes flow as a state of being totally absorbed in an activity. There is no preoccupation with outcomes or worries about failing. The past and future do not exist. One often loses track of time and space. A person in this flow state is working intuitively, and it often seems as if the poem writes itself or the painting just appears.

I often like to go out into the woods and other natural areas with my camera. While I do understand shutter speeds and aperture settings, I have found that I do my best work when I let go of the need to make "good" pictures. Preoccupation with the end product, how the photo will turn out, takes me out of the moment. I may even make a judgment about the worth of the image and talk myself out of taking the photo altogether.

Hart (2000) suggests, "In the normal waking state awareness is subservient to analysis, the possibility of full participation in the event is often thwarted by the expectation of evaluation of it, and deep contact is prohibited by chronic categorizing of the other" (p. 31). Instead I try staying present with where I am, allowing myself to become fascinated with the way the light illuminates the leaves on the trees. I suddenly become aware of all of the small animals, birds, and insects that make their homes in these trees. And I am filled with a deep sense of reverence.

New Directions for Adult and Continuing Education • DOI: 10.1002/ace

Songwriters, artists, dancers, and other creative people do their best work when they tap into their emotional states of joy, grief, fear, or confusion. We make connections to this work from our own emotional states, which provoke and stimulate learning.

Limitations of Language

Language is one-way communication. Although words can provoke feeling responses, they tell us how we should feel leaving nothing open to interpretation; thus, words can be manipulative. Ortega y Gasset (1975) tells us, "One might say whereas language speaks to us of things, merely alluding to them, art actualizes them" (p. 147). Accordingly, "painting begins its communicative task where language leaves off" (p. 199).

Elsewhere I have pointed out the limitations of overdependence on cognition and argued that artistic ways of knowing help us to experience the world in more holistic ways that deepen understanding of self, others, and the world around us (Lawrence, 2005a). The arts do not merely enhance life; they embody it (Goldberg, 2001).

The arts invite a conversation with the viewer or witness. A painting, a poem, a dance can stir up emotion as it touches something deep inside us. Perhaps we connect to a personal experience of our own, or we tap into empathic connections with issues of universal concern, that is, the horrors of violence or the destruction of the earth. Sometimes we are not sure where our strong emotional reactions come from. Experiencing, being with the emotion, resisting our temptation to run from it can open up opportunity for tremendous growth and learning. Thomas Moore (2004) speaks of dark nights of the soul: deep, intense, prolonged experiences of sadness, grief, or disturbance. He suggests creative expression as a way to explore these feelings at a deeper level: "Whatever impulse moves us to create or listen to a mournful song is the same impulse that begs for poetic expression of our dark feelings" (p. 14). According to Moore, these explorations often provide opportunities for transformation.

One way we privilege language over other forms of expression is through the practice of labeling. According to photographer Freeman Patterson (1987), "Labeling, which is seeing with words, interferes with pure observation—with seeing things as they are" (p. 142).

Once we put a label on something, we think we understand it and stop looking any further. For example, we might say, "This is a maple tree. I know maple trees. They have pointy-shaped leaves. In the Midwest, they turn vivid colors in the fall." We may be able to recite facts about maple trees, but have we actually seen the tree? What is the texture of the bark? What does it look like up close? What is the relationship of that tree to others in the forest? How is this particular tree unique?

When I walk through a museum or art gallery I deliberately avoid looking at the titles of paintings or sculptures because reading the title narrows the focus to looking for what the artist wanted me to see rather than trusting my own intuition and knowledge. Viewing art becomes more of an intellectual exercise. Not knowing the title frees me to experience the art in my own way. I feel it, absorb it, allow myself to be drawn into it in spontaneous ways. I pay attention to emotions that are stirred and connections that are made.

As a class activity, I sometimes ask my students to listen to a musical selection in a foreign language, such as "Paite Rima," a Zimbabwean call-and-response prayer for ending the bloodshed. Because we cannot understand the words, our attention focuses on the tone, rhythm, and mood. While lyrics can be powerful, they tell us how we should view the song rather than allowing us to have our own experience. This is another illustration of the limitations of language.

Affective Learning Through the Arts in Theories of Adult Learning

This section explores the role of emotion and creative expression through three theoretical constructs: transformative, experiential, and indigenous learning.

Emotion in Creative Expression and Benefits to the Transformative Learning Process. Since Mezirow (1978) introduced transformative learning to the field of adult education, others have expanded on his ideas. Dirkx (2006) is particularly noted for elaborating on the emotional components of the transformative process. In the past five years, more and more researchers have been exploring the role of the arts in promoting transformative learning in the context of emotionally laden issues.

O'Neill (2004) gave lantern boxes to a group of women who self-identified as having undergone a personal transformation and asked them to artfully depict their journey. She displayed the completed artwork in an installation called Holding Flames. O'Neill believes that women's creative expression is critical for a sense of well-being and self-knowledge. The women in her study found the process of creating the lanterns to be transformative and liberatory. O'Neill says that "art is a potentially emancipatory alternative to formal accepted epistemologies, subverting made-made language and established patriarchal and imperialistic academic traditions" (p. 189).

Simpson (2007) studied men and women who turned to creative expression after experiencing a "disorienting dilemma," as defined by Mezirow (1978). These intense emotional experiences included divorce, cancer, alcoholism, and job loss. During their darkest moments, these individuals turned to journal writing, collage, theater, performance poetry, and graphic arts. Art allowed them a way to move through the transformation in the ways to which Thomas Moore (2004) alluded.

Cueva (2007) used reader's theater (a form of storytelling written in script form like a play that is designed to be read aloud by multiple voices) as a way to promote cancer education. Her study revealed that reader's

New Directions for Adult and Continuing Education • DOI: 10.1002/ace

theater is a nonthreatening way to provoke discussion around this taboo subject and invited participants to explore their own relationship with cancer. She shared her research findings in a play where a character called Feelings talked about how he felt emotionally connected to the dialogue. Another character, called Transformation, talked about how the reading allowed her to experience alternative perspectives.

Lawrence and Butterwick (2007) have been exploring popular theater as a way to heal from oppression through the sharing of stories and the exploration of affective and embodied knowing. Through the acting out of the oppressive circumstances, we can begin to imagine alternative realities and write new stories with more positive outcomes. In doing so, we become agents for personal and collective transformation.

The arts are also a powerful way for communities to bring about transformation and healing. In 1989, Noris Binet, an artist and sociologist, emigrated from the Dominican Republic to Nashville, Tennessee. In an effort to find a creative and meaningful way to heal racial wounds between the Black and White women in her community, she started a project called Black and White Women Building a Bridge, which used visual art, poetry, music, and dance as a medium for antiracist work. This project turned out to be a powerful transformative experience for the women who participated. Binet, however, wanted to extend the opportunity beyond the original group. She wrote a book about the experience, *Women on the Inner Journey* (1994) because

> it is my strong desire to create . . . space in which the reader can become engaged in each of the different steps and be a part of it, too. Why? Because this project is about a process of transformation that is life; never finished, never complete, never perfect. It is about being alive, about nurturing, sharing, supporting, touching, dancing, creating, laughing, reaching out, building bridges, healing wounds, becoming fully human [p. xvii].

Rethinking Experiential Learning Through the Arts and Affective Knowing. Experiential learning is another theoretical construct from which we can explore the role of emotion in learning through art. Experiential learning opportunities are present in both the creating and the witnessing of art. To learn from experience requires one to be fully in the experience: mind, body, heart, and soul. According to Burnard (1988), "The experiential domain of knowledge is knowledge gained through direct personal encounter with a subject, person, place, or thing. It is the subjective and affective nature of that encounter that contributes to this sort of knowledge" (p. 128).

Interestingly, there is no mention of the affective component in the best-known theories of experiential learning. For example, Kolb (1984), a prominent experiential learning theorist, believes that learning occurs through cycles of concrete experience and reflective observation, which leads to the development of new knowledge that can then be applied to new experiences. This theory implies that the learning takes place through reflection, a cognitive and rational process of making sense of an experience that has already occurred.

Feminist scholar Elana Michelson (1998) critiques this assumption, which she sees as an example of abstract masculinity that separates the mind from the body. She recounts an incident of a female manager who is ignored and discounted when she tries to speak up in meetings. The woman becomes angry, her body tenses, and her cheeks feel warm. She later processes the experience on her train ride home. Michelson argues that the actual learning occurred in the moment of feeling the intense emotions and bodily sensations during the experience, not later when she reflects: "Learning is understood as a moment of emotional and physical response [to experience] not a moment of dispassionate self-reflection, as the product of an embodied, social selfhood rather than of a disembodied mind" (p. 226). This assertion supports the notion that the cognitive and affective domains of knowing are intertwined and inseparable. It also implies that somatic and affective ways of knowing precede cognition. Our bodily sensations clue us into our cognitive state: we feel "butterflies" in our stomach and recognize this as anxiety. Our heart races, and we register it as fear. Once we have this knowledge (we have experienced it), we engage in reflection to understand our experience in the context in which it occurs.

Heron (1996) introduced presentational knowing as a way of making sense of experience in an inquiry process. Presentational methods may include poetry, dance, mime, storytelling, drawing, and other art forms. "The inquiry group," Heron states, "becomes an artist's collective, demonstrating art as a mode of knowledge, giving powerful access to the pre-predictive extralinguistic world which phenomenologists tend to write about too much in an analytic mode" (p. 90). Co-inquirers engage in these artistic processes and reflect on their meaning. These methods are used in tandem with propositional forms, which include verbal communication used to analyze and theorize.

The arts offer numerous opportunities for experiential learning. Watching a play or a film or listening to a musical composition may enrage us or move us to tears. We may not even initially understand where the strong emotion is coming from. These emotional reactions can be viewed as opportunities to go deeper. As we reflect on the nature of our response to the film or song, we can gain greater insight into ourselves and the world.

Integrating the Arts Through Mind, Body, Heart, and Spirit: Indigenous Learning. Sometimes the information that we need to solve problems or work toward transforming self and the world in which we live lies just beyond our reach. Opportunities for transformative learning are available to us, but often veiled or hidden. We can access this hidden knowledge by paying attention to imagery that presents itself through dreams and other creative and intuitive processes such as metaphor, story, art, dance, poetry, photography, meditation, and quiet contemplation (Lawrence, 2005b).

Symbol and imagery expressed in dreams, stories, and the arts are an integral part of indigenous education. Unlike Western culture, where art is seen as a specialization or specific area of expertise, indigenous people view all individuals as imaginative and fully creative human beings (Cajete, 1994). In ancient times, everyone created art. There was no distinction between artists and nonartists: "Art was viewed as an expression of life and was practiced, to one extent or another, by all the people of a tribe" (Cajete, 1994, p. 153). Even today, artistic expression is a primary mode of education for indigenous people that is interconnected with their spiritual beliefs and practices. The arts are integral to the ritual and ceremony that are important aspects of indigenous culture.

Cajete also views the role of art in indigenous education as transformative learning. He sees art as an alchemic process that transforms raw materials into an artistic creation and at the same time transforms the artist: "The ceremony of art touches the deepest realms of the psyche and the sacred dimension of the artistic creative process. This is the level that not only transforms something into art but also transforms the artist at the very core of being" (p. 154). Cajete sees the creating of art as a "path to wholeness" (p. 158), not only for the artist but also for those who come in contact with the artistic creation.

Indigenous learning theory is a useful construct to view the interconnected dimensions of cognitive, spiritual, and affective knowing that are inherent in artistic processes. Native American educator Paula Underwood (1994) used the metaphor of strands in a braid to show how mind, body, and spirit, three wisdom traditions, are all necessary for learning: "Each alone may easily unravel, two may be twisted to offer more possibilities and will still unravel, but three fixed firmly at each end—bound by memory and laced with curiosity—such braids truly last!" (p. 17). Underwood's educational practice included the use of learning stories. These simple and eloquent stories, handed down through the generations in Underwood's family, were designed to engage the listener and invite inquiry. The lesson is in the questions.

The Role of the Arts in Educating for Social Justice

The arts have always played a prominent role in education for social change both inside and outside formal institutions. We read about the war in Iraq, global warming, the abuse of children, and other stories in newspapers and watch these stories on our televisions. These communication channels give us information, but it is art that has the power to provoke emotional responses that inspire us to take action.

Wilber (1996) believes that the meaning of art lies simultaneously in the conscious or unconscious intention of the creator, the viewer, and the art itself. The meaning of art is also constructed by the history or context in which it was created or interpreted.

Spehler and Slattery (1999) challenge the dominant assumption that the arts exist primarily for aesthetic purposes. They consider artists to be prophets in the process of social change: "Prophetic poets, visual artists, dancers, actors, lyricists and novelists challenge us to investigate—not ignore—such despair, injustice and paralysis" (p. 2). They go on to explain, "The development of the prophetic voice is a process involving psychological, spiritual, cognitive and emotional aspects of our being" (p. 7).

I believe this interconnectedness of mind, body, heart, and spirit is true for the artist as well as those interacting with the art. It is only when we are deeply affected by an issue that we become motivated to work for change. The arts are a powerful way to bring about that response.

Protest music has long been a vehicle for bringing people together to raise awareness and promote community solidarity. Olson (2005) believes that community music can play a strong role in promoting emancipatory learning among marginalized groups. Phil Ochs was a strong voice throughout the 1960s and early 1970s. His provocative lyrics inspired a generation to think more deeply about the atrocities of war, poverty, and civil disobedience. "Is There Anybody Here?"* speaks to us of the grim realities of war.

Is there anybody here who'd like to change his clothes into a uniform
Is there anybody here who thinks they're only serving on a raging storm
Is there anybody here with glory in their eyes
loyal to the end, whose duty is to die
I wanna see him
I wanna wish him luck
I wanna shake his hand, wanna call his name
Put a medal on the man.
Is there anybody here who'd like to wrap a flag around an early grave
Is there anybody here who thinks they're standing taller on a battle wave
Is there anybody here like to do his part
soldier to the world and a hero to his heart
I wanna see him
I wanna wish him luck
I wanna shake his hand, wanna call his name
Put a medal on the man
Is there anybody here proud of the parade
who'd like to give a cheer and show they're not afraid
I'd like to ask him what he's trying to defend
Oh I'd like to ask him what he thinks he's gonna win
Is there anybody here who thinks that following the orders takes away the blame
Is there anybody here who wouldn't mind a murder by another name
Is there anybody here whose pride is on the line
with the honor of the brave and the courage of the blind
I wanna see him
I wanna wish him luck
I wanna shake his hand, wanna call his name
Put a medal on the man

*"Is There Anybody Here" by Phil Ochs. 1966 Barricade Music, Inc. All rights administered by Almo Music Corp./ASCAP. Used by permission. All rights reserved.

These lyrics, written during the Vietnam War era, could be just as true today. Set to music, they are even more powerful. Today's artists, like Ani DiFranco, Tracy Chapman, and some rap lyricists, are inspiring yet another generation to wake up and take action.

The beat poets of the 1950s such as Allen Ginsberg and Lawrence Ferlinghetti were inspirational in challenging people to question mainstream political practices in the post–World War II era when America feared communism. Black-clad bearded youth gathered in coffee houses where provocative poetry was spoken to the beat of bongo drums. The act of performing the poetry had a much more powerful effect than merely reading it. Today, poetry slams and other types of performance poetry provoke people to look at themselves, the world, and what can be done to bring about change.

Performance ethnography is a form of critical pedagogy that Denzin (2003, p. 16) refers to as a "politics of resistance." He sees performance as a form of cultural resistance to the oppressive structures that surround us. Performing the text makes it public, and it becomes real to us. Witnessing performance ethnography allows one to experience the feelings of the performers and feel empathy for them. We know something about their situation. Denzin states that "*knowing* refers to those embodied sensuous experiences that create conditions for understanding. . . . Thus performed experiences are the sites where felt emotion, memory, desire and understanding come together" (p. 13). Understanding can create an emancipatory discourse that offers hope for a better future.

Guerrilla theater or street theater is a proactive way to get people's attention and teach about critical social justice issues. Soyini Madison, an African American woman living and doing research in Ghana, staged a protest march as a street performance to highlight issues of poverty and human rights facing the people there. Madison (2005) spoke of her work as a "pedagogy of possibility": "I hoped the performance would offer its audience another way to speak of rights and the origins of poverty that would then un-nestle another possibility of informed and strategic action" (p. 538).

I am reminded of my own college days during the Richard Nixon era when the Street Corner Society, a guerilla theater group, performed on the streets of East Lansing, Michigan. Whether their message was women's reproductive issues, gay rights, or antiwar sentiments, one could not help but become caught up in the moment and be moved to work toward change.

Art has long been part of community-based education programs. For example, ArtSpirit, a New York–based organization, is dedicated to encouraging intercultural awareness and healing through artistic expression. One of its projects, The Soup Kitchen Drumming and Art Group, brings together impoverished and homeless individuals with artists and community volunteers from varied backgrounds to drum and engage in art projects such as mask making and other creative activities. The creative process invites informal dialogue focused on understanding difference.

New Directions for Adult and Continuing Education • DOI: 10.1002/ace

Visual art is perhaps the best-known form of expression used to disturb and provoke. For example, Picasso's *Guernica,* painted in 1937 as a political statement depicting the Nazi bombing during the Spanish Civil War, shows the violence and brutality from the perspective of the victims. Educators today still use it to provoke inquiry into the nature of war and conflict.

Installation artist Gerda Meyer Bernstein escaped from Nazi Germany as a child, where many of her family members perished in the concentration camps. Her work, often depicting the atrocities of genocide, torture, sexual exploitation of women, and other hate crimes, is large, often filling a room. To experience Bernstein's work, one must walk through it, thus becoming fully immersed in the experience. *Marginalized* depicts twenty-two female corpses arranged in a circle on a military parachute. *Hooded March* consists of a wall with three doors labeled "Men," "Ladies," and "Colored." Three large crosses lay against the wall. Large white shrouded hoods hang from the ceiling. White sheets contain words like "No dogs or Jews allowed." Another chronicles racist atrocities and murders, including the names of the cities where they occurred. Still another names those who have been lynched, tortured, or otherwise murdered (Fassbinder, 2006). It is impossible to walk through Bernstein's installations and not be deeply affected. We feel the sadness, the horror, and the fear in ways that reading about these events could never provoke.

Much of art for social change is designed to disturb, upset the status quo, and wake us up to noticing what is wrong in the world. Sometimes the same effect can be achieved through images of hope. Artist, activist, and Catholic nun Mary Southard does just that. *Women Singing Earth* depicts a group of women from diverse races and ethnic groups reaching their arms skyward toward an image of the earth. The painting personifies her belief in the power of women from across the globe to rise up and heal the earth. As Maxine Greene (1955) so eloquently states, "Imagining things being otherwise may be a first step toward acting on the belief that they can be changed" (p. 22).

The Emotional Experience of Witnessing Art

Malchiodi (2002) observes, "Art stimulates both those who make it and those who witness it. Creating, imagining and witnessing all instill you with a new sensibility about how you experience yourself in the world" (p. 33).

Throughout this chapter, I have emphasized that learning takes place through the affective experiences of creating art and in encountering art created by others. This section more fully explores the role of the witness who is also a participant in the artistic process. Our response to viewing an art exhibit, watching a play, or listening to a musical composition is always

New Directions for Adult and Continuing Education • DOI: 10.1002/ace

subjective, mediated by our cultural background and previous experiences—our life history. Witnessing art expands our worldview by taking us to new places and allowing us to enter into the lifeworld of another. According to Greene (1995), "The role of imagination . . . is to awaken, to disclose the ordinarily unseen, unheard, and unexpected" (p. 28).

Experiencing the arts can also create a stronger identification with our own cultural history such as a walk through the Holocaust Museum in Washington, D.C., or seeing the history of American slavery depicted at the DuSable Museum of African American History in Chicago. This identification often emerges through a strong emotional reaction to the subject matter and the way it is portrayed. In a study on the aesthetic experiences of museum professionals viewing works of art, Csikszentmihalyi and Robinson (1990) found that 90 percent of their participants reported some level of emotional involvement, and 25 percent said that emotion was their primary mode of response to the art. These emotional reactions were both positive and negative. Once we become aware of our reactions to experiencing the arts, we can begin to engage in dialogue about them to explore the nature of the anger, fear, or joy that was evoked, thus deepening our knowledge.

Implications for Adult and Continuing Education

Learning is a holistic process that involves cognitive, affective, somatic, and spiritual dimensions. The arts naturally engage us in all of these learning domains.

Much of the learning through the arts discussed in this chapter is informal. The teachers are paintings, plays, poetry, and other creative works. Adult educators can tap into the experiential learning of their students by creating opportunities to surface this knowledge. In addition, we can provide our students experiences to create or witness art as part of the curriculum. As Greene (1995) cautions, however, merely being exposed to art is not sufficient to change lives. As we begin to unpack these emotionally charged experiences, we expand the process of critical reflection beyond the cognitive realm by creatively imagining alternative possibilities. Cajete (1994) suggests, "Such practices help students to establish a connection with their real selves and learn how to bring their inner resources to bear in their lives" (p. 225).

Today the word *literacy* means much more than fluency in reading and writing. We hear about information literacy, health literacy, visual literacy, and other kinds. Affective learning through art expands our understanding of literacy as a more holistic, inclusive way of knowing.

To be effective adult educators, we need to take advantage of all of the resources available to us. Tapping in to the deep well of emotion generated by participating in artistic processes as creator or witness and collectively examining the meaning of those emotional experiences can help us to envision alternative realities for a more promising future.

References

Allen, P. B. *Art Is a Spiritual Path*. Boston: Shambhala, 2005.

Binet, N. *Women on the Inner Journey*. Nashville: James C. Winston Publishing Company, 1994.

Burnard, P. "Experiential Learning: Some Theoretical Considerations." *International Journal of Lifelong Education*, 1988, 7, 127–133.

Cajete, G. *Look to the Mountain: An Ecology of Indigenous Education*. Skyland, N.C.: Kivaki Press, 1994.

Csikszentmihalyi, M. *Creativity: Flow and the Psychology of Discovery and Invention*. New York: HarperCollins, 1996.

Csikszentmihalyi, M., and Robinson, R. E. *The Art of Seeing*. Malibu, Calif.: J. Paul Getty Museum and Getty Center for Education in the Arts, 1990.

Cueva, M. "Reader's Theatre as Cancer Education." Unpublished doctoral dissertation, National-Louis University, 2007.

Denzin, N. K. *Performance Ethnography: Critical Pedagogy and the Politics of Culture*. Thousand Oaks, Calif.: Sage, 2003.

Dirkx, J. "The Power of Feelings." In S. B. Merriam (ed.), *The New Update on Adult Learning Theory*. New Directions for Adult and Continuing Education, no. 89. San Francisco: Jossey-Bass, 2001.

Dirkx, J. "Engaging Emotions in Adult Learning." In E. W. Taylor (ed.), *Teaching for Change: Fostering Transformative Learning in the Classroom*. New Directions for Adult and Continuing Education, no. 109. San Francisco: Jossey Bass, 2006.

Fassbinder Fine Art. "Bearing Witness: Gerda Meyer Bernstein." Chicago: Fassbinder Fine Art, 2006.

Goldberg, M. *Arts and Learning*. New York: Addison Wesley Longman, 2001.

Greene, M. *Releasing the Imagination: Essays on Education, the Arts, and Social Change*. San Francisco: Jossey-Bass, 1995.

Hart, T. "Inspiration as Transpersonal Knowing." In T. Hart, P. Nelson, and K. Puhakka (eds.), *Transpersonal Knowing*. New York: SUNY Press, 2000.

Heron, J. *Co-operative Inquiry*. Thousand Oaks, Calif.: Sage, 1996.

Kolb, D. *Experiential Learning*. Upper Saddle River, N.J.: Prentice Hall, 1984.

Lawrence, R. L. "Knowledge Construction as Contested Terrain: Adult Learning Through Artistic Expression." In R. L. Lawrence (ed.), *Artistic Ways of Knowing*. New Directions for Adult and Continuing Education, no. 107. San Francisco: Jossey-Bass, 2005a.

Lawrence, R. L. "Hidden Dimensions of Transformative Learning: Dreamwork, Imagery, Metaphor and Affect Expressed Through Experiential Painting." Paper presented at the Sixth International Transformative Learning Conference, East Lansing, Mich., 2005b.

Lawrence, R. L., and Butterwick, S. "Re-Imaging Oppression: An Arts-Based Embodied Approach to Transformative Learning." Paper presented at the Seventh International Transformative Learning Conference, Albuquerque, N.M., 2007.

Madison, D. S. "Critical Ethnography as Street Performance." In N. K. Denzin and Y. S. Lincoln (eds.), *The Sage Handbook of Qualitative Research*. Thousand Oaks, Calif.: Sage, 2005.

Malchiodi, C. A. *The Soul's Palette: Drawing on Art's Transformative Powers for Health and Well-Being*. Boston: Shambhala, 2002.

Mezirow, J. *Education for Perspective Transformation*. New York: Center for Adult Education, Teachers College, Columbia University, 1978.

Michelson, E. "Re-Membering: The Return of the Body to Experiential Learning." *Studies in Continuing Education*, 1998, 20(2), 217–233.

Moore, T. *Dark Nights of the Soul*. New York: Gotham Books, 2004.

Olson, K. "Music for Community Education and Emancipatory Learning." In R. L. Lawrence (ed.), *Artistic Ways of Knowing*. New Directions for Adult and Continuing Education, no. 107. San Francisco: Jossey-Bass, 2005.

O'Neill, E. "Holding Flames: Women Illuminating Knowledge of S/Self-Transformation."
In E. O'Sullivan and M. Taylor (eds.), *Learning Toward an Ecological Consciousness.*
New York: Palgrave Macmillan, 2004.

Ortega y Gasset, J. *Phenomenology and Art.* New York: Norton, 1975.

Patterson, F. *Portraits of Earth.* San Francisco: Sierra Club Books, 1987.

Simpson, S. "Dancing All of Life." Unpublished doctoral dissertation, National-Louis
University, 2007.

Spehler, R. M., and Slattery, P. "Voices of Imagination: The Artist as Prophet in the
Process of Social Change." *International Journal of Leadership in Education,* 1999, 2(1),
1–12.

Underwood, P. *Three Strands in the Braid: A Guide for Enablers of Learning.* San Anselmo,
Calif.: Tribe of Two Press, 1994.

Wilber, K. "Transpersonal Art and Literary Theory." *Journal of Transpersonal Psychology,* 1996, 28(1), 63–91.

Wuthnow, R. *Creative Spirituality.* Berkeley: University of California Press, 2001.

RANDEE LIPSON LAWRENCE *is an associate professor in the Department of Adult
Education at National-Louis University.*

8

*Emotions play a key role in teaching in nonformal edu-
cational settings. Developing an awareness of learner
emotions and their relationship to nonformal learning
experiences is an essential practice for the nonformal
educator.*

Teaching and Emotions in a Nonformal Educational Setting

Edward W. Taylor

Little is known about the nature of teaching and the role of emotions in
nonformal education. This is not surprising, given that nonformal education has many shades of meaning, limited literature exists about the realities of teaching in nonformal settings, and little has been written about the
nature of emotions and teaching in formal settings, let alone nonformal settings. Despite these shortcomings, an emerging body of work is beginning
to shed light on the unique nature of nonformal education as a practice and
an educational setting that can potentially stimulate a whole range of emotions. If emotions and their role in learning are better understood by the
nonformal educator, the result could be more effective practice. As Meredith,
Fortner, and Mullins (1997) suggest, "There is both professional opinion
and empirical research which suggest that the major advantages of learning
activities in nonformal settings over those in formal settings may lie in the
affective domain" (p. 806). To set the context for this chapter, I begin with
a brief vignette of a nonformal educational event that I observed at a local
home improvement store.

Nonformal Education: A Case Example

Midmorning on a Saturday at a hardware store, an employee named Betty
was preparing to teach a clinic on laying ceramic tile. She had set up a work
table near the rug and tile center next to a major thoroughfare of the store.
On the table were all the supplies of her trade (grout, mastic, sponges, and

NEW DIRECTIONS FOR ADULT AND CONTINUING EDUCATION, no. 120, Winter 2008 © 2008 Wiley Periodicals, Inc.
Published online in Wiley InterScience (www.interscience.wiley.com) • DOI: 10.1002/ace.318

so on), types of tile, and the beginnings of a tile-laying project. A big sign was set up to notify interested customers when the clinic was going to start. Around 11:00 A.M., people began to gather around the table.

Betty introduced herself and immediately began to engage the learners. She projected herself as someone who was excited and feeling positive (smiling) about the workshop and confident about laying tile. She assured her learners that laying tile is fun and rewarding, and with the right planning, anyone can do it. Soon after introducing herself, she assessed the crowd by asking learners individually what brought them to the clinic and what kind of tile projects they were working on. She made a concerted effort to listen and explain how their needs would be addressed.

Following an assessment of the learners' needs, she started the workshop by explaining what could be expected from the clinic and identifying all the items on the work table. Some of the more interesting tools, such as the trowel and bullnose tile, were passed around for learners to handle and look at more closely. All the while, Betty maintained eye contact, smiled, and regularly assessed the learners' reactions to her presentation. She was having fun, used humor, at times making fun of her own missteps in laying tile that could be easily corrected, and at the same time staying on task, as if there were a clock ticking somewhere reminding her how little time she had with these learners.

As the clinic continued, the crowd grew to the point of partially blocking the thoroughfare; something was pulling them into the clinic from the margins. The nonformal educational event was like a sponge, grabbing the attention of store customers as they walked by. They were intrigued, attentively listening to Betty's demonstration. At the same time, there was a trickle of learners who were leaving the clinic, presumably because they were no longer interested, had other tasks to complete in the store, or had gotten the information they needed and moved on. As the participation level shifted, Betty started to get the learners more engaged as if aware that she might be pushing their level of interest. She asked for volunteers to come to the table to experience laying tile on recently spread mastic (glue), all the while addressing questions that seemed to pull the clinic in various directions. Appearing at ease, Betty moved the clinic along, answering questions despite the fact that new learners to the clinic would ask questions that she had addressed earlier in the session.

Eventually interest peaked, and the learners, who had been standing during the entire presentation, began to squirm and shuffle their feet and became less attentive and more restless from standing still so long. More and more learners were peeling off from the crowd, no one was asking more questions, and the learners were less focused. It was these affective signs that prompted Betty to bring the clinic to a close. She ended by encouraging everyone to try tile laying at home, and she made herself available to meet with people individually at the end of the clinic if they had additional questions. Within a span of roughly thirty minutes, the clinic ended and the crowd dispersed.

Nonformal Education

This case example illustrates a nonformal educational event: an episode of teaching and learning that goes on in a variety of settings (museums, state parks, community education centers, cooperative extension, and consumer education sites) every day throughout this country. Nonformal education is often referred to as a "motley assortment of organized and semi-organized educational activities operating outside the regular structure and routines of the formal [educational] system, aimed at serving a great variety of learning needs of different subgroups in the population young and old" (Ahmed and Coombs, 1975, p. xxix). It is generally defined in relationship to formal education as both "not formal education" (Norland, 2005, p. 6) and the opposite of formal education.

Nonformal education is typically described as more focused on the present, learner centered, less structured, and responsive to localized needs, and there is an assumed nonhierarchical relationship between the learner and the nonformal educator (Ahmed and Coombs, 1975; Bock and Bock, 1989; Courtney, 1991; Ewert, 1989; Jarvis, 1987; Marsick and Watkins, 1990; Merriam and Caffarella, 1999; Reed and Loughran, 1984), even though recent research (Taylor, 2006) has questioned some of these long-held beliefs about nonformal education. In addition, a variety of teaching challenges exists in a nonformal education setting that are generally not found in formal educational settings. For example, time for teaching is short in duration; participation is generally voluntary; there is often a wide variety of abilities and ages among learners; there are often regular distractions, such as noise and interruptions, in nonformal settings, particularly in outdoor and public settings; and educational personnel are often hired to teach for their content expertise and may have little systematic teacher training. It is these and other challenges that are unique to the nonformal setting, impacting learning and providing a context for eliciting a range of emotions from both the nonformal educator and the learner.

Framing Emotions Within a Nonformal
Educational Setting

One approach to help make sense of emotions in a nonformal setting, such as Betty's home improvement clinic, is to use a framework by Sutton and Wheatley (2003) for conceptualizing emotions in practice. They understand emotions as multicomponent processes that consist of a number of subsystems (network of changes) of the individual: the components of appraisal, subjective experience, physiological change, emotional expression, and action tendencies that both influence each other and are somewhat independent.

Appraisal is the beginning of the emotional process, where there is an interpretation of "some transaction in terms of its significance or relevance for the individual's motives, goals or concerns" (Sutton and Wheatley, p. 329). Three characteristics make up appraisal that is significant for experiencing emotions: goal relevance (the degree it relates to personal goals), goal congruence (more congruent results in more positive emotions and less so for negative emotions), and ego involvement (the degree of personal benefits and harm in relationship to others). For example, Betty successfully accomplished her goals and received supportive feedback (learners were engaged, interested), which elicited positive feelings from the learners about this nonformal educational experience. Appraisal also sheds light on the subjective experience of emotions, such that not everyone appraises an experience similarly. Cultural and personal differences exist in how both the educator and the learner assess an educational experience. Similarly, those who experience joy while teaching in a nonformal setting have a different experience teaching from those who experience anxiety and stress.

The third and fourth components of the emotional process are physiological changes (for example, in body temperature, heart rate, blood pressure) and emotional expressions (facial expression and tensing of the body, for example), which often "occur in predictable ways when an individual experiences emotions" (p. 331). These components are observed and reacted on by the educator and consciously felt by the learner. For example, Betty's excitement about the clinic, expressed through positive facial expressions and a relaxed manner, stimulated learners' interest. Also, the visitors' restless behavior at the end of the clinic reflected a growing feeling of boredom and lack of interest.

The last component is action tendencies, or responses to emotions. These tendencies often are modulated and controlled by contextual constraints (social and cultural mores). For example, Betty may have been frustrated with the lack of involvement by the customers in the tile-laying demonstration, but due to the public nature of the nonformal educational event and the overall goal of the clinic, it is unlikely that she would have expressed her frustration openly to the group of learners. Furthermore, she used humor to help the learners feel more relaxed, minimizing ego involvement (personal risk) and increasing the likelihood of their participation. This framework is helpful because it provides shared discourse for making sense of emotions in practice, although it does not go far enough in explaining what is unique about the nonformal educational setting.

Context, Nonformal Educator, and Learner

To understand the nature of emotions within a nonformal setting, it is important to discuss its unique context and the impact it has on the affective

New Directions for Adult and Continuing Education • DOI: 10.1002/ace

experience of teachers and learners as they engage each other in this setting. The nonformal context poses a number of challenges that provide a catalyst for a variety of emotions. The contextual factors that seem most influential are the nature of participation, such as free choice and voluntary participation (Falk, 2001; Falk and Dierking, 2002); the novel setting (Bitgood, 1988); temporal constraints (Taylor, 2006); and the heterogeneity found among learners, such as age, class, and social background (Busque, 1991; Falk, Koran, and Dierking, 1986). How the nonformal educator responds emotionally to these demands determines to a great extent the success of the educational experience.

For example, a significant challenge when teaching in a nonformal setting is free choice (Falk, 2001; Falk and Dierking, 2002). This is where the learner has the choice to attend or not attend (physically and mentally) an educational event. This freedom of choice demands that the nonformal educator provide an educational experience that captures the learners' attention so they choose to attend. As a result, the nonformal educator must regularly appraise the learners' emotive state, checking for goal congruence, feedback, and level of interest, much more so than would be expected within a formal educational setting, where often the teacher has a captive audience. The nonformal educator must create an education event that attracts "the attention of the visitor and [holds] attention long enough to communicate its intended message" (Meredith, Fortner, and Mullins, 1997, p. 808). In addition, once the learner is involved, without continual awareness (appraisal) of the learner's attention level, the nonformal educator would have little understanding of how to respond if and when the learner's interest dissipated and why he or she might have chosen to leave the educational event. Consequently, the presence of free choice for many nonformal educators creates anxiety (particularly in less experienced educators), compromising cognition and limiting the available mental resources to respond to the myriad of everyday nonformal educational challenges (Eysenck and Calvo, 1992).

Free choice has emotional implications for the learner as well. In voluntary settings, learners often have a heightened sense of curiosity and attention to newness. For example, in a tour of an art museum, it is the selective attention of the learner that determines if he or she will view a particular painting or pay attention to the tour guide's discussion of a sculptor. A significant influence on the selective attention and involvement of the learner is his or her motivational state. Celsi and Olson (1988) refer to this motivational state as "felt involvement" (p. 211), a feeling of personal relevance for an object or an event. Felt involvement is a by-product of two sources: one being situational and immediate (the physical and social aspects that emerge in the museum itself that promote learner involvement) and the other being that which involves the intrinsic characteristics of the learner (a product of past experiences and related to personal goals and values). For example, a learner who was an art major might demonstrate enduring (highly engaged) involvement during a tour of an art museum.

However, the level of involvement will also be situational due to the power (expertise) of the nonformal educator and the type of art in the museum.

The significance of novelty and the influence on visitors also shed light on the relationship between emotions and learning. This is particularly the case in museums and parks, where there are opportunities to learn in situ in the original setting or a close fabrication. These nonformal settings can be described as having an authentic presence. The emotional power of the novel setting is brought to life by Courtney's (1995) description of his visit to the Sixth Floor Museum in Dallas, the location where Oswald was when he shot President Kennedy: "It is an authentic context for learning. . . . However, there is no gainsaying of the profundity of the emotion you experience as, unrestrained by person or barrier, you approach one of a number of windows which affords a would-be assassin barely interrupted visual passage to the street and plaza below" (p. 4).

In novel settings, the context often speaks for itself, and the nonformal educator plays an adjunct role, interpreting and highlighting key contextual cues to maximize the emotive nature of the experience. Even Betty's clinic on tile laying has an authentic presence since it is situated in a location where the materials are sold and customers often engage in discourse of how these materials are used.

Temporal constraints are another contextual factor unique to the nonformal setting that has significant influence (Taylor, 2006): the limited amount of time the nonformal educator has with the learner and the limited opportunity for repeated engagement with the learner. Most nonformal educational events are short in duration, and rarely do educators see the learner beyond one learning event. Successful nonformal education experiences on the surface seem to be unstructured, situated, and responsive to the local conditions, with little attention to time. However, research has shown that across a variety of nonformal settings, educators seem to adhere to a deeply rooted structure that is very much bounded by time (Taylor, 2006).

For educators, this contextual factor has a number of affective implications. Every time they begin a nonformal program, they are confronted with a new group of learners, often heterogeneous in background. As a result, if they are going to provide a successful educational experience, they have to develop rapport with the learners within a limited amount of time. Emotionally this can be stressful, creating a sense of being under pressure to complete a task (covering prescribed content) and at the same time finding a way to connect with the learners. Recent research has shown that in response to these contextual factors, nonformal educators place a great deal of emphasis on promoting a feeling of fun and less on learning a particular body of knowledge. Modeling a desired behavior, such as positive feelings, through fun, "can be effective in increasing participation in museum exhibits, thus influencing the selective attention of visitors, particularly adults" (Celsi and Olson, 1988, p. 808).

New Directions for Adult and Continuing Education • DOI: 10.1002/ace

Time is also a factor for learners. Attention and curiosity are fleeting phenomena, particularly in free choice settings, where learners can disengage mentally from a presentation or move on to other activities they find more interesting. In addition, there are physiological factors, such as the consequence of standing in one location for an extended period of time. If a nonformal event such as a tour is not emotionally engaging by promoting curiosity and attention and runs over a long period of time, learners will feel bored (yawn) and restless (shuffle their feet) as described in the vignette at the beginning of this chapter. These behaviors are indicators of learners' emotions and levels of interest in relationship to the nonformal educational event. A nonformal educator who can properly appraise and address them in a timely manner can often rectify them, resulting in a more successful educational experience.

Implications for Practice

Based on the analysis of the nonformal education context from an affective perspective, it is apparent that nonformal educators face a number of unique emotional challenges. In response to these challenges, several strategies have been identified that will help educators promote greater felt involvement by the learner in the educational experience.

First, it is important to model behaviors and emotions that are desired among learners who are participating in the nonformal educational event. This means that the nonformal educator must project positive feelings about both the learners and the teaching event, increasing the likelihood that they will reciprocate in kind. Projecting positive emotions helps draw learners into the experience and assists in maintaining their interest. Furthermore, a positive and supportive affective environment helps minimize ego involvement (risk) and creates a secure and safe feeling among learners, increasing the likelihood of greater visitor participation.

Second, educators need to be constantly using assessment, a process of both ascertaining learner needs and establishing a rapport. Research has shown that many successful nonformal educators begin an educational experience by exploring why learners have chosen to attend the event (Taylor, 2006). Understanding the learner interests provides an opportunity for the nonformal educator to explore ways to make connections between the educational experience and the learners' interests, leading to greater felt involvement by the learners. Furthermore, demonstrating an interest in the learner needs, along with engaging them on a personal level (if time allows), helps to establish rapport by being in sync emotionally with the learners and establishing a comfortable and supportive environment for learning.

Third, it is important to develop an acute awareness of the learners' emotional states at the beginning and throughout the event. For nonformal educators, this requires a heightened sense of appraisal, continually assessing the learners' emotional state (felt involvement) by observing their level of eye contact, verbal interaction, and body language. Nonformal educators need to ask themselves whether the learners look interested and engaged. If not, and if instead they appear restless and bored and are not focused on the nonformal educational experience, the educator needs to respond accordingly by looking for ways to quickly promote curiosity and selective attention through novelty and learner participation.

Fourth, it helps to be conscious of time and aware of the emotional impact that time has on the learners and the educational experience. Often due to the limited amount of time available, nonformal educators feel pressured to cover as much material as they can as quickly as possible. The consequence of an emphasis on content often leads to less-than-successful educational experiences for the learner. Learners lose interest quickly in a lengthy didactic presentation, particularly if it lacks opportunities for questioning and active engagement. Through planning, nonformal educators need to identify what is most important for the learners and allow time for their personal involvement in the experience.

Fifth, the educational experience should be fun. In a recent case study of two nonformal sites, one of the most interesting findings was the "high degree of emphasis on fun by nonformal educators" (Taylor, 2006, p. 302). Fun explains to a great extent why learners attend nonformal educational events. Such events generally foster positive emotions of pleasure, excitement, and joy. However, promoting fun is a challenging skill, and not all educators have the wherewithal and knowledge of how to plan for fun, particularly within such demanding learning environments as nonformal settings. In response to this challenge, advice from successful practicing nonformal educators suggests the need to find a way to make the teaching of the nonformal educational experience fun for themselves. Without that, there is little likelihood it will be fun for the learners.

Conclusion

When promoting successful nonformal educational experiences, it is important to remember to give serious attention to the affective domain. By being responsive to the learners' emotions first and foremost, nonformal educators are likely to engage the learners, maintain their interest, and ensure a positive nonformal learning experience.

References

Ahmed, M., and Coombs, P. H. (eds.). *Education for Rural Development.* New York: Praeger, 1975.

Bitgood, S. "Environmental Psychology of Museums, Zoos, and Other Exhibition Centers." In R. Bechtel and A. Churchman (eds.), *Handbook of Environmental Psychology.* San Francisco: Jossey-Bass, 1988.

Bock, J. C., and Bock, C. M. "Nonformal Education Policy: Developing Countries." In C. J. Titmus (ed.), *Lifelong Education for Adults: An International Handbook.* New York: Pergamon Press, 1989.

Busque, L. "Potential Interaction and Potential Investigation of Science Center Exhibits and Visitors' Interest." *Journal of Research in Science Teaching,* 1991, *28,* 411–421.

Celsi, R. L., and Olson, J. C. "The Role of Involvement in Attention and Comprehension Processes." *Journal of Consumer Research,* 1988, *15*(2), 210–224.

Courtney, S. "Defining Adult and Continuing Education." In S. B. Merriam and P. M. Cunningham (eds.), *Handbook of Adult and Continuing Education.* San Francisco: Jossey-Bass, 1991.

Courtney, S. "The Sixth Floor: Museum Experiences as Learning Environments." 1995. The University of Nebraska-Lincoln, Lincoln. (ED 413 517)

Ewert, D. M. "Adult Education and International Development." In S. B. Merriam and P. M. Cunningham (eds.), *Handbook of Adult and Continuing Education.* San Francisco: Jossey-Bass, 1989.

Eysenck, M. W., and Calvo, M. G. "Anxiety and Performance: The Processing Efficiency Theory." *Cognition and Emotions,* 1992, *6,* 409–434.

Falk, J. H. (ed.). *Free-Choice Science Education.* New York: Teachers College Press, 2001.

Falk, J. H., and Dierking, L. D. *Lessons Without Limits.* Lanham, Md.: Rowman and Littlefield, 2002.

Falk, J. H., Koran, J. J., Jr., and Dierking, L. D. "The Things of Science: Assessing the Learning Potential of Science Museums." *Science Education,* 1986, *70,* 503–508.

Jarvis, P. *Adult Learning in a Social Context.* London: Croom Helm, 1987.

Marsick, V. J., and Watkins, K. E. *Informal and Incidental Learning in the Workplace.* London: Routledge, 1990.

Meredith, J. E., Fortner, R. W., and Mullins, G. W. "Model of Affective Learning for Nonformal Science Education Facilities." *Journal of Research in Science Teaching,* 1997, *34,* 805–815.

Merriam, S., and Caffarella, R. S. *Learning in Adulthood.* San Francisco: Jossey-Bass, 1999.

Norland, E. " 'The Nuances of Being "Non': Evaluating Nonformal Education Programs and Settings." In E. Norland and C. Somers (eds.), *Evaluating Nonformal Education Programs and Settings.* New Directions for Evaluation, no. 108. San Francisco: Jossey-Bass, 2005.

Reed, H. B., and Loughran, E. L. (eds.). *Beyond Schools: Education for Economic, Social and Personal Development.* Amherst, Mass.: Community Education Resource Center, 1984.

Sutton, R. E., and Wheatley, K. F. "Teachers' Emotions and Teaching: A Review of the Literature and Directions for Future Research." *Educational Psychology Review,* 2003, *15,* 327–358.

Taylor, E. W. "Making Meaning of Local Nonformal Education: Practitioner's Perspective." *Adult Education Quarterly,* 2006, *56,* 291–307.

EDWARD W. TAYLOR is an associate professor in the adult education program in the School of Behavioral Sciences and Education at Penn State University–Harrisburg.

9

In this chapter, the authors reflect on the ways in which the preceding chapters contribute to a deeper understanding of the role of emotions in adult learning.

The Emotional Self in Adult Learning

M. Carolyn Clark, John M. Dirkx

So how do you conclude a volume on emotions and adult learning? One idea that occurred to us was to provide a conversation about the book itself. John, of course, is the insider here, since this is a topic both dear to his heart and about which he has written extensively (Dirkx, 2001, 2006), and this book is shaped by his interest in the topic and evolving ideas about it. Carolyn is the outsider, but a friendly one. She comes with several perspectives and interests that complement this topic, particularly embodied learning and narrative learning (Clark, 2001; Rossiter and Clark, 2007; Clark and Rossiter, 2006), and she and John share an interest in the self and the various and evolving ways in which that concept is understood (Clark and Dirkx, 2000). We hope our conversation here build on the ideas so well articulated by the chapter authors of this book:

CAROLYN: John, I think you should lead off here. What contribution do you see this volume making to our understanding of the complex connections between emotions and learning in adulthood?

JOHN: What we have between the covers of this book is an alternative way of thinking about the role of affect and emotion in teaching and learning in adult, continuing, and higher education. The chapter authors clearly demonstrate that while teaching and learning are experienced in particular ways within particular contexts, these experiences all share powerful emotional dimensions that help shape and influence the meaning of these experiences for teachers and learners alike. These accounts help us better understand the meaning of emotion in settings of adult learning. Emotion is not something that simply invades our experiences of teaching and

NEW DIRECTIONS FOR ADULT AND CONTINUING EDUCATION, no. 120, Winter 2008 © 2008 Wiley Periodicals, Inc.
Published online in Wiley InterScience (www.interscience.wiley.com) • DOI: 10.1002/ace.319

learning, an alien force trying to mess up our best-laid plans and intentions, a manifestation of our weak character or ability to control our emotions. Rather, through the expression of affect and emotion in adult learning, we are offered a kind of language for reinterpreting ourselves and the possibility to experience and recreate our sense of selves, our subjectivities, our being-in-the-world.

CAROLYN: I definitely agree with what you are saying, but frankly I have to admit that my first reaction after reading this book was less to agree with all that was said and more to be puzzled that this topic needs to be addressed at all. Education is a human enterprise, and both learners and educators are fully human. It takes an act of imagination to conceive of a human being who does not have an emotional life. I am reminded of the character that Anthony Hopkins played in the movie *The Remains of the Day*, a butler to a British lord in the 1930s who was a supporter of Hitler. Hopkins's character represses all his emotions in order to maintain what he considers to be the identity of the perfect butler, unflinchingly loyal to his employer. Emma Thompson, the new housekeeper, tries to draw out his humanity and fails utterly. I especially remember the scene late in the movie where Thompson is in her room, sobbing uncontrollably because of her inability to reach this man whom she has come to care for. Unexpectedly Hopkins appears at her door with a work-related request. Thompson and the audience are suspended for a long dramatic moment, hoping that seeing her profound distress will be the emotional turning point for him— but he instead ignores what is happening before him and woodenly proceeds with the household business that brought him there. It is the response of an automaton, not that of a fully human being. It is an extraordinary dramatic moment precisely because it flies in the face of our socially accepted definition of what it means to be human. As I said, it takes an act of imagination to conjure up a person devoid of emotion. How is it that we as educators, and more particularly those of us in the West, do not take it as a given that we and our students are emotional as well as physical and rational beings? I think someone from a non-Western culture would find this completely puzzling.

We know the answer, of course, and a number of the authors in this book make reference to it. We in the West live in a dualistic world. For my money, I think Descartes has a lot to answer for. The mind-body dualism that he set forth has become a fundamental assumption of Western thought, and it has wrought havoc and continues to do so, despite the challenges of feminist and postmodern thought. And I think we see it in our own field. Books like this one are a corrective to this distorted thinking of what it means to be human. Randee's chapter on arts-based learning is a particularly good example of making the argument for so-called alternative modes of learning. John, you yourself argue against this dualistic notion in your opening chapter when you talk about moving away from thinking about emotions as baggage to be dealt with in the learning process to a more holistic understanding of learning. But it is a shame that we have to be engaged in this corrective process at all.

JOHN: Carolyn, I agree that it is a little disheartening to have to explicitly draw attention to the critical role of emotions in the processes of learning and meaning making. Unfortunately, the more integrated and holistic perspectives reflected in the accounts presented in this volume are not widely shared within the field. We have a ways to go before educators recognize emotions in adult learning, especially so-called negative emotions, as something other than a barrier or challenge to effective learning experiences, something to get off one's chest before real learning can occur.

Your recounting of that scene from *Remains of the Day* provides a chilling account of the centrality of emotions in human relations but also the power of the so-called rational, ego-centered self to suppress their expression in the everydayness of our lives. It underscores for us and dispels any illusions about the difficulty of developing constructive relationships with the emotional self. While Emma openly grieves for what will not be, the butler himself is locked within his own private hell. When in education we fail to recognize the emotional dimensions of our learners' experiences and how these emotions are integral to the fabric of the meaning of their experiences, we too are guilty of fostering a deep slip in our learners' understandings of the self.

Let me suggest some themes suggested by the chapter authors regarding the different ways that emotions play a positive and constructive role in teaching and learning. The settings for adult learning reflected in these chapters range from adult basic education to learning through the arts and in home improvement centers. In each case, this emotional dimension of teaching and learning stretches beyond a focus on the individual alone, reflecting within its forms of gladness, pain, loss, desire, and longing the play of the social and the cultural. The learners' personal experiences of emotion cannot be fully understood apart from their contexts. The joys and sorrows of adult basic education students struggling with the challenges of literacy are intimately interconnected with the social and economic conditions of their past and current lives. The adult learner in higher education is often haunted by feelings from past educational experiences of not measuring up or not being good enough, yet surprised by the joy of his or her current success. Some women seeking to further their education find great comfort in supportive partners, while other women are beaten for their aspirations. To speak of the emotional dimensions of teaching and learning, several authors also need to articulate the political, economic, and cultural conditions in which these forms of adult learning occur. The personal is also political.

The narratives contained within this volume suggest that the experience of emotion reflects the complex relationships of the psyche, the body, and the social and cultural contexts that shape and form the lives of learners and teachers. Rather than emotion being something that subverts or

obstructs understanding, it seems to provide a means of more fully grasp-
ing the wholeness of one's experience. Allowing students to give voice to
powerful affect is not getting it off their chests and getting it out of the way,
but encouraging them to own and integrate these feelings and emotions
within their sense of being.

In each of these chapters, emotion and the emotional self are manifest
in differing ways. For example, Janet Isserlis implies in Chapter Two that
learning in adult basic education cannot be fully understood without attention to the underlying trauma and violence that characterize the lives of so
many of the participants. Caught in and surrounded by life conditions that
seem to often spiral out of control, learners in adult basic education programs seem further victimized by governmental policies and agencies that
are interpreting these contexts from an increasingly functionalist perspective. In contrast to the often desperate contexts of these learners, Carol E.
Kasworm outlines in Chapter Three the hopes that guide the lives of returning adult learners in higher education. Out of the complex and sometimes
contradictory conditions, Kasworm argues, hope arises in various forms.
Reflecting the challenges of their current lives, these forms of hope also
express what learners grasp as the possible, extending itself into their
futures.

Emotions in learning are also bound up with working across difference. For example, Regina O. Smith argues in Chapter Four that the
emotional experiences of adult learners in online collaborative environments express the deeper and often unconscious dynamics that characterize self-other relationships. These dynamics reveal how the learners'
perceptions of their identity as group members are intimately bound up
with their emotional experiences of difference within these contexts. Lisa
M. Baumgartner and Juanita Johnson-Bailey also suggest in Chapter Five
that powerful emotions are associated with the experience of difference,
but they locate these experiences more concretely around race and White
privilege. When teachers raise such issues, they are often met with sharp
and powerful emotional responses from their learners, which may evoke
difficult emotions among teachers themselves. Learning to work across difference, they argue, involves working through such feelings as anger, grief,
and sadness.

The political and cultural dimensions that Baumgartner and Johnson-
Bailey stressed are also suggested by Laura L. Bierema's analysis in Chapter
Six of emotion in workplace learning and its relationship to worker and
organizational well-being. Her analysis stresses the emotional context of
work and organizational life, and how the concept of emotional intelligence
has fueled attention to emotion labor, particularly within certain kinds of
occupations and organizations. This idea of emotion labor illustrates ways
in which the political, the social, and the personal intersect within given
emotional contexts of work. As in the case of Bierema's Disney employees
and the home improvement instructors that Edward W. Taylor discusses in

Chapter Eight, employees are expected to manage contradictory emotions, display socially desirable emotions even when they are not feeling these emotions, and suppress those not consistent with the expectations of their role.

Taylor and Randee Lipson Lawrence in Chapter Seven point out that nonformal and informal contexts for adult learning also reflect important emotional dimensions of teaching and learning. Taylor points to the different contexts for nonformal learning and the need for educators to assess and appraise the learners' emotional states. In these contexts, marked by their open structures and the freedom for learners to come and go at will, Taylor illustrates how emotion plays a role in learners' decisions, as well as in the educators' choices of methods and strategies. Emotion management seems critical to the work of educators in nonformal education, as it is with airline flight attendants.

Lipson Lawrence extends this analysis of learning outside the classroom to informal learning in and through the arts, suggesting that imaginative engagement evoked in and through the arts also reflects learners' deep emotional engagement. Through the powerful emotions associated with this play of the imagination, whether in dance, poetry, story, or the visual arts, learners often experience deeper and perhaps less visible aspects of their selves. While Taylor stresses the more conscious and cognitive dimensions of emotion in nonformal learning, Lipson Lawrence, similar to Smith in online learning, draws our attention to the somewhat hidden dimensions and expressions of emotion in nonformal learning.

Implicit in these narratives is the relationship of emotion to the self and self-identity, or what we are referring to here as the emotional self. To embrace a constructive role of emotions in adult learning is to recognize the powerful role that emotions play in both the meaning we make of our lives and the ways in which we construct that meaning. This form of adult learning involves what Lupton (1998) refers to as emotion work, a concept also suggested by Bierema in this volume. While Bierema focuses on the impression management role of emotion work, Lupton suggests that emotion work is integral to the realization of one's emotional self. But what does it mean to work on one's emotions? What does it mean to recognize this powerful role of emotions in adult learning and to do emotion work within the context of learning environments?

For Lupton (1998), how we explain and understand our emotional experiences represents "part of the continuing project of subjectivity" (p. 169). This evolving emotion work also involves the development of a deeper sense of how acculturation within specific sociocultural contexts shapes our emotions, a point elaborated by Baumgartner and Johnson-Bailey, and a growing recognition of how these experiences are intimately bound up with physical sensations within our bodies, supported by Lipson Lawrence's discussion of the role of art and imagination in nonformal learning.

For Lupton, emotion work involves "management and experience of the emotional self . . . , including unconscious and semi-conscious habituated action as well as highly conscious and calculated strategies" (p. 168). Thus, emotion work involves, paradoxically, both a kind of emotional management and an emancipation of emotional expression, an idea that resonates both implicitly and explicitly throughout the chapters in this volume. We come to increasingly recognize the various emotions that comprise our learning experiences by attending to our bodies, our sociocultural contexts, and our own subjectivities. Their expression within our learning becomes an integral aspect of our learning.

This emotion work also involves some of the management strategies Goleman (1995) suggested in the idea of emotional intelligence. In doing emotion work, we learn to distinguish between the appropriate contexts for expressing or containing our emotions. Lupton (1968) points out, "Being a 'civilized' person in terms of the presentation of the emotional self means being cognizant of when it is appropriate to repress the expression of one's feelings and when it is appropriate to reveal them, and act accordingly" (p. 172).

The literature in adult and continuing education suggests ways in which teachers and learners can incorporate emotion work in processes of adult learning. In addition to some of the strategies that the chapter authors suggest, others have explored additional ways to frame this work, such as whole person learning (Yorks and Kasl, 2002, 2006) and imaginal methods (Dirkx, 2001, 2006).

CAROLYN: John, you do a fine job of drawing together the various threads of these chapters and weaving them together to give us something new to consider. Your words have altered my original thoughts about work on emotions in learning being largely or even primarily a corrective to our Western dualistic thinking. Now I am beginning to see that the contributions in this book, as well as by other scholars cited, serve to open a door to the complexities of the relationship between emotion and learning in adulthood, complexities ignored by my earlier statement that what we are engaged in here is a corrective process. I think it would be more accurate to describe this as a complex process of exploration and discovery, of problematization of cultural norms and assumptions, of challenging earlier understandings and beliefs, all centering around the fully human experience of learning situated in different, changing, even unstable social locations.

In our postmodern age (or post-postmodern, as some argue), I think we have a moral obligation as adult educators to complexify (if I can coin a term) our study of how all adults learn in the fullness of our humanity. The intersection between learning and the emotional dimension of our lives is a critically important place to engage that complexity, and I believe this book takes an important step in that scholarly process.

References

Clark, M. C. "Off the Beaten Path: Some Creative Approaches in Adult Learning." In S. Merriam (ed.), *The New Update on Adult Learning Theory*. New Directions in Adult and Continuing Education, no. 89. San Francisco: Jossey-Bass, 2001.

Clark, M. C., and Dirkx, J. "Moving Beyond a Unitary Self: A Reflective Dialogue." In A. L. Wilson and E. R Hayes (eds.), *Handbook of Adult and Continuing Education*. San Francisco: Jossey-Bass, 2000.

Clark, M. C., and Rossiter, M. "'Now the Pieces are in Place . . .': Learning Through Personal Storytelling in the Adult Classroom." *New Horizons in Adult Education and Human Resource Development*, 2006, 20(3), 19–33.

Dirkx, J. M. "The Power of Feelings: Emotion, Imagination, and the Construction of Meaning in Adult Learning." In S. B. Merriam (ed.), *The New Update on Adult Learning Theory*. New Directions for Adult and Continuing Education, no. 89. San Francisco: Jossey-Bass, 2001.

Dirkx, J. M. "Engaging Emotions in Adult Learning: A Jungian Perspective on Emotion and Transformative Learning." In E. Taylor (ed.), *Fostering Transformative Learning in the Classroom: Challenges and Innovations*. New Directions in Adult and Continuing Education, no. 109. San Francisco: Jossey-Bass, 2006.

Goleman, D. *Emotional Intelligence: Why It Can Matter More Than IQ*. New York: Bantam Books, 1995.

Lupton, D. *The Emotional Self: A Sociocultural Exploration*. Thousand Oaks, Calif.: Sage, 1998.

Rossiter, M., and Clark, M. C. *Narrative Learning and the Practice of Adult Education*. Malabar, Fla.: Krieger, 2007.

Yorks, L., and Kasl, E. "Toward a Theory and Practice for Whole-Person Learning: Reconceptualizing Experience and the Role of Affect." *Adult Education Quarterly*, 2002, 52(3), 176–192.

Yorks, L., and Kasl, E. "I Know More Than I Can Say: A Taxonomy for Using Expressive Ways of Knowing to Foster Transformative Learning." *Journal of Transformative Education*, 2006, 4(1), 43–64.

M. CAROLYN CLARK *is associate professor of adult education at Texas A&M University.*

JOHN M. DIRKX *is professor of higher, adult, and lifelong education at Michigan State University.*

INDEX

Ackerman, R. H., 58
Adams, M., 46
Adult education programs: facilitating adult learners, 20–23; government policies on basic, 19–20; implications of arts-based affective knowing for, 75; strategies for engaging adult learners, 23–25. *See also* Education; Nonformal education
Adult educators: classroom interactions in context of race and, 48–49; examining the practices of, 47–51; facilitating group learning collaboration, 41–42; nonformal education context of, 82–85; online group role played by, 37–38; on resistance to antiracist education, 50–51; response to marginalized student classroom interactions, 49–50
Adult learner challenges: adult education programs responding to, 20–25; examining the emotional, 27–33
Adult learners: academically underprepared, 19–25; classroom interaction by marginalized, 49–50; classroom interactions in context of race by, 48–49; considering future possibilities, 32–33; continuing in college through renegotiation or adaptation, 29–32; entering college to succeed, 27–29; nonformal education context of, 82–85; personality conflicts among, 9–10; resistance to antiracist education by, 50–51; special challenges faced by, 20–23, 27–33; strategies for engaging, 23–25. *See also* Employees
Adult learning: for the academically underprepared, 19–25; emotion and alternative ways of knowing in, 15–16; emotion and workplace, 56–59; the emotional self in, 14–15, 35–42, 89–94; implications of online groups for, 41–42; transformative learning process introduced for, 68–69; whys in which emotion is manifested in, 9–11; in the workplace, 55–62. *See also* Learning
Adult Literacy Professional Development Discussion List, 22

Ahmed, M., 81
Allen, I. E., 35
Allen, P. B., 66
Alvin Ailey American Dance Theater, 65
Antiracist education, 50–51
Art: to disturb and provoke, 74; emotional experience of witnessing, 74–75; integrating arts through indigenous, 70–71; interconnectedness definition of, 72; rethinking experiential learning through, 69–70; social justice education through, 71–75
Arts-based affective knowing: building the case for, 65–67; implications for adult and continuing education, 75; limitation of language overcome by, 67–68; transformative learning process of, 68–69. *See also* Knowing
ArtSpirit, 73
Ashforth, B. E., 58
Attention spans, 85

Bailey, T., 29
Barlas, C., 13
Barry, L. L., 58
Baumgartner, L. M., 2, 3, 8, 11, 13, 14, 15, 45, 47, 53, 92, 93
Beard, C., 15
Bennis, W. G., 36, 38
Berg, D. N., 36, 37
Bernstein, G. M., 74
Bierema, L. L., 3, 55, 64, 92
Binet, N., 69
Bitgood, S., 83
Black and White Women Building a Bridge project, 69
Bock, C. M., 81
Bock, J. C., 81
Boshier, R., 35
Boud, D., 15
Boulton, G., 35
Bowen, A. E., 61
Boyd, R. D., 15, 16, 40
Brookfield, S., 8, 10, 52
Brotheridge, C. M., 57
Bruffee, K. A., 36, 37, 38
Burard, P., 69

97

NEW DIRECTIONS FOR ADULT AND CONTINUING EDUCATION
ORDER FORM SUBSCRIPTION AND SINGLE ISSUES

DISCOUNTED BACK ISSUES:

Use this form to receive 20% off all back issues of *New Directions for Adult and Continuing Education*.
All single issues priced at **$23.20** (normally $29.00)

TITLE	ISSUE NO.	ISBN
_____	_____	_____
_____	_____	_____
_____	_____	_____

*Call 888-378-2537 or see mailing instructions below. When calling, mention the promotional code JB9ND
to receive your discount. For a complete list of issues, please visit www.josseybass.com/go/ndace*

SUBSCRIPTIONS: (1 YEAR, 4 ISSUES)

☐ New Order ☐ Renewal

U.S.	☐ Individual: $89	☐ Institutional: $228
CANADA/MEXICO	☐ Individual: $89	☐ Institutional: $268
ALL OTHERS	☐ Individual: $113	☐ Institutional: $302

*Call 888-378-2537 or see mailing and pricing instructions below.
Online subscriptions are available at www.interscience.wiley.com*

ORDER TOTALS:

Issue / Subscription Amount: $ _____

Shipping Amount: $ _____
(for single issues only – subscription prices include shipping)

Total Amount: $ _____

SHIPPING CHARGES:

First Item	$5.00
Each Add'l Item	$3.00

*(No sales tax for U.S. subscriptions. Canadian residents, add GST for subscription orders. Individual rate subscriptions must
be paid by personal check or credit card. Individual rate subscriptions may not be resold as library copies.)*

BILLING & SHIPPING INFORMATION:

☐ **PAYMENT ENCLOSED:** *(U.S. check or money order only. All payments must be in U.S. dollars.)*

☐ **CREDIT CARD:** ☐ VISA ☐ MC ☐ AMEX

Card number _____ Exp. Date _____

Card Holder Name _____ Card Issue # _____

Signature _____ Day Phone _____

☐ **BILL ME:** *(U.S. institutional orders only. Purchase order required.)*

Purchase order # _____
　　　　　　　　Federal Tax ID 13559302 • GST 89102-8052

Name _____

Address _____

Phone _____ E-mail _____

Copy or detach page and send to: **John Wiley & Sons, PTSC, 5th Floor
989 Market Street, San Francisco, CA 94103-1741**

Order Form can also be faxed to: **888-481-2665**

PROMO JB9ND

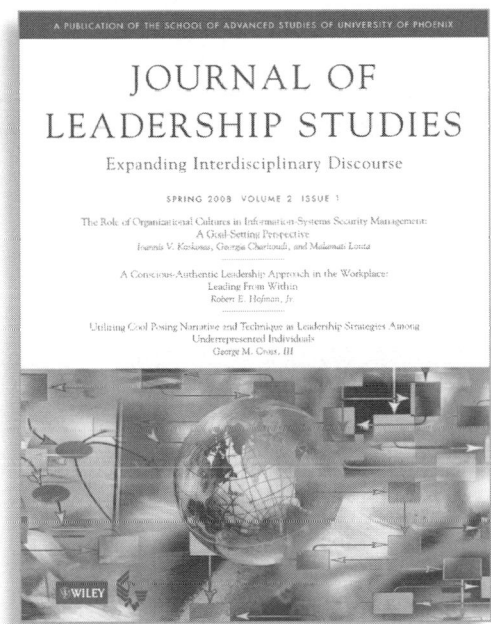

Why Wait to Make Great Discoveries

When you can make them in an instant with Wiley InterScience® Pay-Per-View and ArticleSelect™

Now you can have instant, full-text access to an extensive collection of journal articles or book chapters available on Wiley InterScience. With Pay-Per-View and ArticleSelect™, there's no limit to what you can discover...

ArticleSelect™ is a token-based service, providing access to full-text content from non-subscribed journals to existing institutional customers (EAL and BAL)

Pay-per-view is available to any user, regardless of whether they hold a subscription with Wiley InterScience.

Benefits:

- Access online full-text content from journals and books that are outside your current library holdings
- Use it at home, on the road, from anywhere at any time
- Build an archive of articles and chapters targeted for your unique research needs
- Take advantage of our free profiled alerting service the perfect companion to help you find specific articles in your field as soon as they're published
- Get what you need instantly no waiting for document delivery
- Fast, easy, and secure online credit card processing for pay-per-view downloads
- Special, cost-savings for EAL customers: whenever a customer spends tokens on a title equaling 115% of its subscription price, the customer is auto-subscribed for the year
- Access is instant and available for 24 hours

WILEY InterScience®
DISCOVER SOMETHING GREAT

www.interscience.wiley.com

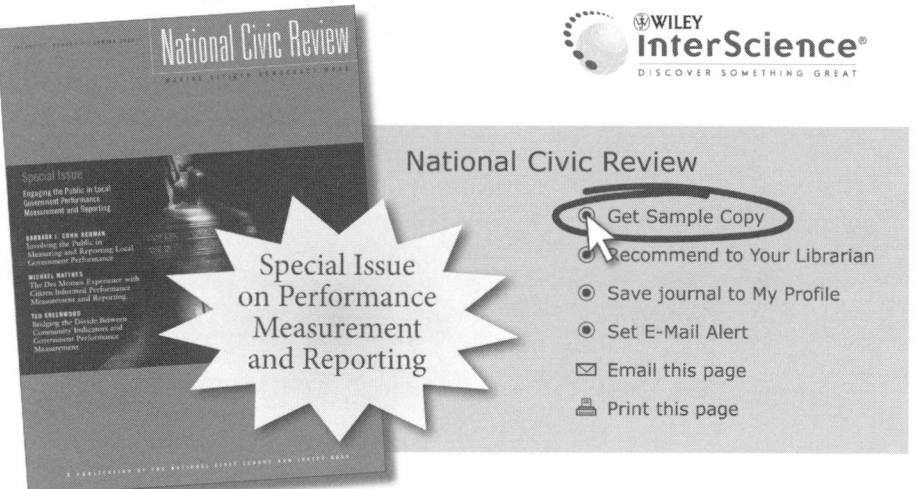